SPLAT!

TONY DAVIS

SPLAT!

The madness and magnificence
of the world's most dangerous sports

ARENA
ALLEN&UNWIN

First published in 2007

Arena, an imprint of
Allen & Unwin
83 Alexander Street
Crows Nest NSW 2065
Australia
Phone: (61 2) 8425 0100
Fax: (61 2) 9906 2218
Email: info@allenandunwin.com
Web: www.allenandunwin.com

National Library of Australia
Cataloguing-in-Publication entry:

Davis, Tony.
Splat!: the madness and magnificence of the world's most dangerous sports.

ISBN 978 1 74175 030 0

1. Extereme sports. 1. Title

796.046

Design and layout by Justine O'Donnell for jmedia, Sydney, Australia
Printed in Australia by McPherson's Printing Group

10 9 8 7 6 5 4 3 2 1

Tony Davis is widely blamed for *Lemon! Sixty Heroic Failures of Motoring*, an Australian bestseller that has been published in the US and UK, and the eccentric literary memoir *F. Scott, Ernest and Me*. His first children's novel—**Roland Wright, Future Knight**—will be released in October 2007. He lives in Sydney, Australia.

Shane McConkey (American Skier, BASE jumper and Sky diver), and Chris Santacroce (American paraglider and ultralight pilot) demonstrate two different methods of finding yourself halfway up a cliff. The action is in Page, Arizona, USA, in 2003.

Photo: Christian Pendella, Red Bull Photofiles

Ross Clarke-Jones on a rolling
mountain of water at Dungeons,
Hout Bay, Cape Town, South
Africa in 2006.

CONTENTS

8

Pilot chute out, boats approaching fast. American BASE jumper Miles Daisher over Trump Marina, Atlantic City, USA.

Photo: Christian Pondella/Red Bull Photofiles

WHY THE HELL WOULD YOU?

Dangerous sports. How does one discuss them with the correct tone? After all, there is something at once marvellously heroic and fabulously daft about sailing great distances through the air on a pair of snow skis, descending 200 metres below the ocean's surface without scuba gear or exceeding the speed of sound in a jet-powered car that looks like an oversized hypodermic needle.

The consequences of anything going wrong can affect the rest of your life, or even end it there and then. And if you get it right, what have you achieved? Have your death-defying exertions advanced humanity a millimetre, fed the starving, cured disease or delivered a single tangible benefit to a single other person?

Of course not. Yet you may have enthralled spectators, transformed yourself, inspired another or even redefined what mankind thought was possible. Magnificent things can be achieved out of any sport, even one that seems completely mad to outsiders, achievements comparable with those of the early explorers who headed off into the farthest reaches of the Earth, or the pioneer aviators who flew into the unknown with machines held together by canvas and baling wire.

To do anything that requires skill and precision better than anyone has ever done it before—or even better than you've ever done it before—can't be worthless. The mere act of putting heart and soul into something that is both difficult and dangerous immediately elevates someone above the millions who coast through life well within their limits, who never find out what it is like to fly, or sail or speed beyond the normal boundaries, and who never pit themselves against another in a contest that affords no second chances.

Yet for all that, there is still something ridiculous about a grown man dressed in tight leather rolling down a big hill while lying on a glorified skateboard, something slightly dippy about a woman trying to ride a tiny board on a wave big enough to capsize an ocean liner, something crazy and even offensive about two men being locked in a cage to test their mixed martial arts' skills.

There's the question, too, of how one categorises dangerous or extreme sports. Which is the riskiest? Well, that depends on the answer you're looking for. After all, according to the NSW Coroner and others, the most mortally dangerous sport in statistical terms is: rock fishing. That will come as no surprise to many fish, but it is deadly for humans too. A remarkably high number of anglers, some of them elderly and unable to swim, are swept off rocks and drown. They weren't courting danger, though. They were just trying to catch some fish. So should we define the most dangerous sports as the ones in which the most people die, the ones in which the most people are hurt, or the ones in which the potential for serious injury is highest? Or perhaps we should give more weight to those sports in which the participants willingly expose themselves to extreme speed and force, or venture out the furthest without a safety net.

Further complicating our quandary is the presence of two distinct categories of dangerous sports. The first contains those sports in which, if everything goes well, you will be uninjured and you can always tell yourself that, if you are skilful and diligent, you will not get injured. BASE jumping is a good example. Some argue—not necessarily convincingly—that if you approach it correctly, a BASE jump is safer than the car trip that takes you to the cliff you are going to leap off.

Into the second category fall those sports where, even if everything goes well and you are skilful and diligent, you'll be horribly bruised and battered. Boxing is the most obvious example: you cannot escape injury if you take part in the sport. And there is something even more remarkable than boxing: amateur boxing. The contestants suffer all the same misery without a single cent of recompense. Some of them aren't even using the amateur game as a stepping stone to a professional career and the chance of big paydays. They just like hitting and being hit.

In choosing the sports included here, I've taken all this into account but have also aimed for interest and variety. There's no point having too many types of motor racing or combat sports, the challenges and dangers remain reasonably similar within each group. And I wanted to capture the action on land, in the sky and at sea, all of them arenas entirely suitable for mayhem and majesty in the name of sport.

There is another interesting division between dangerous sports: those that happen in the public eye and those that take place in lonely, out-of-the-way places. The first offers more opportunities for showing off, in itself sufficient motivation for some people to risk their necks. The second is often attempted for more personal reasons.

Extreme sports were once essentially for men but now women take part in almost all dangerous sports. And in some cases they are chasing outright records. It is less clear whether such sports are becoming more common. Many believe that they are: that modern affluent society has finally reached the point of conquering early death, and is celebrating by somersaulting off cliffs and jumping out of aeroplanes on surfboards. But perhaps this perception is fostered by the video culture that brings new and spectacular varieties of sports so readily into our lounge rooms, and by the marketers who have clamped onto them in the hope of reflected glory for their fizzy drinks or investment funds.

Statistics show high-injury sports such as boxing now have far fewer participants than before, while 'acceptable' sporting activities such as rugby and motor racing have been made safer through stricter rule enforcement and/or better equipment. After the Interlaken tragedy of 1999 (in which 21 young holidaymakers were killed while canyoning), Australian mountaineer Greg Mortimer told ABC radio:

> I really have an alarming sense that, in the last ten years, we've become increasingly concerned about people being killed in the outdoors on adventures … I've got a suspicion that we've become more closeted, that we've become more urbane and a little less able and willing as a community to take some risks and to see our youth take risks.

It is hard to argue with him. As a society we are, by any historical standard, wrapped in cotton wool. We are less likely than ever to be directly involved in war, and our cars are harder to prang due to electronic safety systems—and, when we do hit something, protective bags of air mysteriously pop out of every surface. We watch what we eat and read weather charts and travel warnings before we leave home. We even wear crash helmets as we ride bicycles at low speeds down leafy parkways.

That's why true extreme sportspeople stand out more than ever. They are doing what the majority is prepared to experience only via DVD, ideally in a climate-controlled room. They stand out, too, because their personality type usually means they have to keep exceeding their previous achievements, even when they are already way ahead of the pack. They usually keep going even when all the signs say they should stop.

At nearly 60 years of age, after three serious gorings and a knee replacement, England's only senior matador, Frank Evans, still says he is determined to make a comeback. Motorcycle Grand Prix winner Kevin McGee came out of a coma in 1990 and announced his collision with the tarmac hadn't left him with brain damage and he'd be able to race again. Many thought it was an oxymoron: the fact he wanted to race a Grand Prix motorcycle again only proved McGee did have brain damage.

Dangerous activities generally lend themselves to gallows humour. When the American stuntman of the 1920s to 1960s, Louis 'Speedy' Babbs, was asked if he was afraid he might be killed while pursuing his career path, his reply was, 'Do you plan on leaving this world alive?'

In the end, it all comes down to the rewards versus the risks. The rush of speed and the thrill of victory versus bumps, breaks and bruises, or even death. Those with no interest in balancing such an equation argue that we don't need to take unnecessary physical risks. There's even a theory that those who do are stupid because an intelligent mind puts self-preservation at the top of its list.

Sure, the naysayers may concede an occasional need to put things on the line to create or break empires, to protect our loved ones or to secure food in hard times. But does anyone need to risk everything to be the ninth person to summit an obscure mountain in Pakistan via its southern face? To set a personal best 'No Limit' free dive, or to jump over more buses on a motorcycle? For some, the answer will always be 'Yes, we need to take risks for those things, too'. So to return to the question at the beginning of this introduction: why the hell would you? Here are just a few reasons.

FAME

People who are daring usually grab our attention and the bigger the challenge, the greater the respect and prestige to be won. However, it is becoming harder to stand out. The biggest mountains have been conquered—on a single day in 1993, no less than 39 people stood on the summit of Mount Everest—and there are so many other things vying for our attention. Hence ever more eccentric and edgy feats: people riding off sheer cliffs on BMX bicycles or hurling themselves through the sky with a trebuchet.

Many competitors in extreme sports have long and complex rationales for why they do what they do, but some admit to more basic urges. Few are as upfront as boxer Joe Bugner, who frankly told me he is a 'self-seeking egomaniac', then added, 'Recognition. I love it. It's the fact people recognise my achievements that makes it worthwhile.'

And why boxing? 'You can't show off, you can't put yourself on the line as much in a team sport ... I didn't like to share my glory with anybody.'

Unfortunately, the need to be noticed in sports such as BASE jumping and big wave surfing—both of which are now filmed as a matter of course—can lead to the potentially fatal syndrome known as 'Kodak Courage'.

REAL-LIFE DRAMA

When a racing motorcyclist leans into a high-speed bend on a water-logged circuit, or a freestyle hang-glider pilot commences a full loop perilously close to the ground in an attempt to snatch an against-the-odds victory, what happens next is very much in the lap of the sporting gods.

'This drama is not contrived, it is happening before your eyes,' says Australian sociologist Ian Andrews, 'and sometimes the outcome couldn't be scripted or people would say it was ridiculous.'

Andrews believes that in a world becoming increasingly rational and ordered, 'sport has retained a sense of magic, a sense of mystery.'

There is no doubt that sport at its highest level provides drama, and that being involved as a competitor puts one in the very centre of that theatre.

AESTHETIC CONSIDERATIONS

Many sports have been claimed as graceful, elegant and aesthetically pleasing. David Kirke, the president of Oxford's legendary Dangerous Sports Club, claims risky sporting endeavours are art:

> *It is the photographs and the images that are going to be the tiny legacy we leave behind. And they are a whole lot better than a lot of photographs that are passing for art nowadays. It is no different from any desire of the writer or the poet to leave just a few footprints to mark his brief time on this troubled earth.*

Extreme sport can also provide a metaphor for the best and worst things in life. Charles Nevin wrote in *The Independent* in 2003 of a sport that 'captures much of humanity's high mix of seriousness and farce, grace and brutality, courage and fear, nobility and pointlessness; its need to challenge, to dominate.' He was talking about bull fighting, but the same could apply to many other sports.

ATTRACTING THE OPPOSITE SEX

A willingness to take risks once identified the male who secured the most food and resources. Since we've become 'civilised', the male with the biggest pile of goodies is more likely some personality-free pile of adipose tissue who trades bonds for Deutsche Bank. Yet it seems that, consciously or unconsciously, women

This drama is happening before your eyes, and sometimes the outcome couldn't be scripted or people would say it was ridiculous.

It is really about travelling to the absolute edge of yourself and looking back on it all and being able to say: after all that crap I still managed to get here.

are still attracted to men who are prepared to dice with death. And to some extent men like women who do the same.

There have been many academic papers written on the subject. The study by Jonathan F. Bassett and Brett Moss (2004) probably says it best with its title 'Men and women prefer risk takers as romantic and non-romantic partners'. Bassett and Moss report that both men and women preferred risk takers as friends and short-term romantic partners 'but only women preferred risk takers as long-term romantic partners. The observed gender differences are consistent with predictions from the perspective of evolutionary psychology.'

So don't delay, climb a mountain today.

FINDING LIMITS

This is the motivation most extreme sportspeople admit to: a personal fascination with what the human body is capable of and how hard, or how fast, or how far, a person can push and remain in control. If you do everything within your known abilities, they argue, you learn nothing.

Wing commander Andy Green has driven a jet-powered car at an average speed of nearly 1230 kilometres per hour, in the process becoming the only man ever to set a supersonic land speed record. 'It is part of the human condition,' he says, 'that we push the boundaries, that we try to do things that have never been done before.'

Tanya Streeter, who in the early 2000s blitzed outright free diving world records, says: 'It's about learning about myself and my mental and physical capabilities more than anything else. It just happened to be free diving ... and I just happened to break records. It is really about travelling to the absolute edge of yourself and looking back on it all and being able to say: "after all that crap I still managed to get here."'

Another free diver, Patrick Musimu, explained over the phone from Brussels that he stood on a weighted sled and descended 209.6 metres below the ocean simply because the experts said he couldn't, that his body would literally collapse with the water pressure. 'I knew I was risking my life. But you are just so convinced you can do it, that this is put aside.'

Perhaps the sportsman most in need of finding his personal limits in every field was Göran Kropp, who rode his bicycle from his home in Sweden to Mount Everest, climbed to the summit unaided (and without supplementary oxygen) then packed all his equipment back on his bike and rode home. 'I wanted an adventure that was truly unprecedented,' he said. Kropp's attempt to ski to the North Pole was foiled by frostbite. When he died in a rock-climbing accident in 2002 he was getting ready to sail solo from Seattle to Antarctica, then ski nearly 2000 kilometres to the South Pole and return by the same method.

CAMARADERIE

Working in a small team on a life-and-death matter—whether it be ascending a lofty peak or trying to wring the last few kilometres per hour out of an unpredictable and unforgiving racing machine—is exhilarating and can lead to the sort of lifelong bonds rarely forged outside of war-time. World record-holding BASE jumper Heather Swan undertakes her most ambitious jumps and sky dives with her husband, Dr Glenn Singleman. In her book *Defying Gravity Defying Fear*, Swan wrote:

> You don't need to say much when you share an experience like jumping off a cliff. There is an unspoken bond, an intimacy that reminds us of what we are made of, what we are capable of, when we let down the self-imposed walls that imprison us.

DISCOVERY

The explorer's impulse exists to varying degrees in all of us. George Mallory famously summed up his relentless, and ultimately fatal, need to climb Everest with the phrase 'because it is there'. Mallory also said, 'If you cannot understand that there is something in man which responds to the challenge of this mountain and goes out to meet it, that the struggle is the struggle of life itself upward and forever upward, then you won't see why we go.'

Australian mountaineer Tim Macartney-Snape has explained his love of climbing in terms of the physical pleasure, the mental challenge, the beauty and the closeness to nature. 'But underlying all is the compulsion to explore, to wonder what is possible, where we have come from and where we are going,' he says.

However, although mountains are there, others things aren't. Someone had to think up formation sky diving and, although the snow was there, the ski ramp was not. Perhaps these merely represent the transfer of the explorer's impulse from geography to technology.

WINNING

If high-stakes sport is addictive, winning is even more so. And for some, it is worth chancing their lives. Even after a crash in Italy left him a paraplegic, American motorcycle racing champion Wayne Rainey said, 'I felt if I could win that race, I would win the championship. It was a struggle at that pace, but I couldn't back off. Was first place worth risking almost dying, and losing the ability to walk? I say, 'yes, it was.'

In the same interview (conducted seven months after the accident by Sydney journalist Peter McKay), the remarkable Rainey added:

> I was paid to take risks; hey, I wanted to take risks. When I got hurt, lying in hospital I had no regrets about how I got there. I wouldn't change a thing. I won three world titles. Now I regret I can't take risks, but I don't want anyone to feel sorry for me, 'cause I sure as hell don't.

EXCELLING

Almost every extreme sport requires much more than bravery. Many people gravitate to the sport they can do best, rather than the sport they most want to do, or the sport that is the safest or brings the most money and attention. Tracie Max Sachs says that in trying to beat the world snow-skiing speed record—she has already achieved 238 kilometres per hour—her sole motivation is 'not just trying to be OK at something but trying to be the best that you can be. I don't have a lot to prove to anyone because I'm not sure all that many people are looking.'

DEALING WITH FEAR

Extreme sportspeople are scared by what they do, except those who are merely stupid (and they rarely last long). Fear is a natural reaction to danger and a successful sportsperson needs to have the right balance: enough of it to survive, but not so much they can't excel.

Former world motorcycle racing champion Wayne Gardner sums up the quandary:

> You do have this sense that nothing's going to happen to you, but you've got to believe that because if you rode in your comfort zone, you are never going to win. But at the same time you know you can get hurt, maimed, killed. One of my greatest fears was getting neck or spinal injuries, a Wayne Rainey scenario, and I guess I always had that in the back of my mind, and that was useful because it stopped me being totally reckless.

Noah Johnson, a nuggety surfer from Hawaii, once expressed similar feelings: 'If I wasn't afraid I'd do some really stupid things. The fear is always there.'

When I interviewed him for this book, Dr Glenn Singleman, a man who has leapt from the 6604-metre Meru Peak wearing a wingsuit, cited the most unlikely pay-off—it has helped him with his public speaking:

I was paid to take risks; hey, I wanted to take risks. When I got hurt, lying in hospital I had no regrets about how I got there.

The real benefit of adventure sports: for everyone who undertakes them is that they get in control of their fears. Especially if you are BASE jumping, because one of the most primitive basic instincts is to be scared of heights ...

The real benefit of adventure sports: for everyone who undertakes them is that they get in control of their fears. It is the only way you can do it. Especially if you are BASE jumping, because one of the most primitive basic instincts is to be scared of heights ...

I've got to override that fear with my understanding and knowledge of the technology I'm using, and also my judgement. I will say 'I've had the training, I've got the right equipment, the landing area is good, the weather conditions are right', and therefore I can override the natural fear of jumping off something.

Once you are able to get that level of control, then that level of control spreads out into other parts of your life. Other things that used to be fearful don't have that level of power any more, things like standing up on a stage and speaking ... It is amazing when that happens.

Singleman could have also considered Toastmasters.

Austrian racing driver Niki Lauda surprised almost everyone by surviving the horrific Formula One crash that left him disfigured. He further amazed people by returning to racing only a few weeks later. Several years afterwards he described in an autobiography how he overcame the fear that would still visit him:

What I do is I go off quietly by myself and think things through. What am I afraid of? That I'll make a mistake? I tell myself, no, because I am on top of my job. That something will go wrong with the car? Answer: if I didn't have total confidence in our designer John Barnard and in the McLaren, I would have been with a different team ages ago. No, it won't be mechanical failure. Or am I worried that another driver will cause a shunt? Here I tell myself that I can trust so-and-so and so-and-so and that I'll simply have to keep my wits about me when I'm anywhere near the rest of them. That kind of rationalisation is normally enough to rid me of that queasy feeling.

CEREBRAL WORKOUT

The mental aspect forms an integral part of any sport worth doing. Contestants may be dealing with personal demons (trying to come back after a major injury, for example), trying to out-psyche fellow competitors, or just revelling in pushing their grey matter harder than they have ever pushed it before, perhaps in keeping with the wonderful maxim, 'the more you use your brain, the better it works'. Michael Milton, Australia's fastest skier, says one of the greatest things about his sport is 'standing at the top of a speed skiing track, which is 2 kilometres long on a 70 degree gradient slope and learning how your mind works under pressure, and how to deal with that pressure.'

DISTRACTION

In his book *The Savage God: A Study of Suicide*, English writer Al Alvarez ponders whether he has found the rationale of all risky sports:

You deliberately raise the ante of effort and concentration in order, as it were, to clear your mind of trivialities. It's a small scale model for living, but with a difference: unlike your routine life, where mistakes can usually be recouped, and some kind of compromise patched up, your actions, for however brief a period, are deadly serious.

Greg Mortimer, who with Tim Macartney-Snape was the first Australian to summit Everest, lit up as he explained over a cup of tea that one of the greatest joys of climbing is that:

> You have an immediacy and presence of mind that doesn't just go on for a 90-minute match. It goes on for three months. That's a real luxury in that you have no distractions and the things that are otherwise important to you in your daily life just drop away and no longer seem important. That doesn't mean you love your wife any less but you are required to focus on the day, the here and now.

The theme recurs again and again. Professional surfer Dave Kalama once said: 'the wave commands so much focus and so much attention, it's the only thing that matters for a few seconds, and it's very purifying because as far you are concerned, nothing else exists.'

SHEER BLOODY FUN

Ashley Crick has plummeted to Earth at more than 500 kilometres per hour in a sky diving contest in France, making him probably the fastest non-motorised sportsman of all time. 'After a jump,' he says:

> This drug of some sort, whether it is endorphins I don't know, but this drug is released in your body and you can't describe it until you feel it. That's what you do it for, that feeling of accomplishment and those chemicals released in your body. And then when you get that competition pressure on top of the sky diving itself, it's just enhancing it.

DARKER, STRANGER MOTIVES

A few of the sports covered in this book—most notably boxing and mixed martial arts (MMA)—are unambiguously brutal and can be won only by injuring another person. Bull fighting can end satisfactorily only in death. No matter what they tell you, some contestants must be drawn by a simple love of state-sanctioned physical violence.

Could there be even more to a love of such sports? Texas-based academic Timothy Mitchell, author of *Blood Sport: A Social History of Spanish Bullfighting*, wrote:

> The bullfight is a spectacle of killing and gratuitous risk of life. It is extremely difficult for human beings to engage upon such transgression without being aroused in some way. Even reactions of horror and nausea confirm that violent spectacle is inherently erotic.

Even in non-combative extreme sports, the possibility of death or violent injury makes things far more edgy and strangely compelling. Every single thing in such sports happens with a far greater intensity than you'll ever find in beach volleyball.

So there you have just a few motives. No doubt there are hundreds more, but there's also the possibility that all the grandiose theories about motivation amount to no more than post-purchase justification by people who are hard-wired to do what they do. After talking to extreme sportspeople in many fields, that's my conclusion: almost all the people involved in these sports can't help themselves. If they were denied any so-called logical excuse, or refused payment, recognition or any other outward reward, they would still be engaging in such activities because they have the thrill-seeking gene, the built-in need to experience ever sharper sensations, the irrepressible urge to push themselves harder and harder. And harder and harder.

But enough of the groundwork. Let's take a leap through some of the world's toughest, most dangerous and most unusual sports.

Aerial ballet: the aerial is the A in BASE and here Felix Baumgartner jumps off a large example in Messina, Italy. He is multiply exposed in more ways than one.

1

BASE JUMP ING

OBJECTIVE

To leap off a fixed object and deploy a specially-designed parachute sometime before hitting planet Earth. The later the 'chute is deployed, the better—up to a point, that point being the ground. BASE stands for **B**uilding, **A**ntenna, **S**pan (as in bridge) and **E**arth (as in hill, rock or cliff), and BASE devotees try to achieve at least one hop, skip or jump from each of the four fixed objects, at which point he or she is assigned a BASE number.

REWARDS

Bragging rights and personal satisfaction. There have been only a tiny number of corporate sponsorships or one-off deals to perform in public. There seems to be a requirement that BASE jumpers make documentary films about their exploits. Some of these make money, as does giving motivational speeches to grey and unfit executives who think they can somehow transfer someone else's experience of jumping off an 800-metre cliff into their bold plan to restructure the purchasing department. Most of all, there is morbid glamour. BASE jumpers have taken over the role filled in an earlier time by racing car drivers and test pilots. They are considered the most daring of their breed and the most likely to be dead before your next conversation.

RISKS

Hitting the ground at a speed roughly equalling the acceleration of gravity (that is, about 9.8 metres per second per second). Hitting bits of the object you have just jumped off, or having your parachute snag on something. Potential 'chute problems include non-deployment (usually fatal), partial deployment (major injuries), or bursting (see non-deployment).

WHY?

It is new, it is exciting, it is very much on the edge. The feeling of acceleration is much more dramatic than it is in sky diving, as the ground is so much closer. The stakes are much higher, too, as there is no reserve 'chute and so little time to correct a problem. BASE jumper Heather Swan considers that 'it's got to be one of life's most intense experiences'. And for all the publicity given to the fatalities (more than a hundred since 1981), this should be weighed against the tens of thousands of leaps now being made around the world every year.

WHY NOT?

Extensive preparation is needed for a very short pay-off. Participation can void life insurance policies. It's illegal in many places, so possible arrest is a concern.

The variable legal status also means it is often practised in secret locations, leading to jumpers being horribly injured a long way from help. Perhaps that's why the thesaurus gives such synonyms for 'base' as 'low' and 'vile'.

THE RUNDOWN

The first base jumpers took to the air before the term was coined or the idea was formed that it could be a sport or recreational activity. As long ago as 1912, Austrian tailor Franz Reichelt jumped 60 metres from the first deck of the Eiffel Tower wearing a self-designed overcoat-cum-parachute. Unfortunately, he hit the ground at roughly the same speed as someone wearing no overcoat-cum-parachute and clutching a boat anchor. Reichelt was killed instantly but many people with more effective equipment survived jumps from cliffs and buildings (including New York's World Trade Center) before the modern sport was born.

In 1978, parachutists were filmed jumping off El Capitan, a 915-metre cliff in Yosemite National Park. In 1981 Carl Boenish coined the phrase BASE and began the system of issuing a sequential 'BASE number' to each person who had made a least one jump from each of the four specified types of structure.

Perhaps unaware of what was happening overseas, but driven by the same spirit (and perhaps a desire for publicity), in 1982 three parachutists jumped off the Sydney Harbour Bridge. Unfortunately one was badly injured when his 'chute failed to open. Twenty-five years later injuries and deaths were still making headlines. In May 2006, Tony Coombes, a 30-year-old Queenslander with more than 250 BASE jumps and 1200 sky dives to his credit, plunged to his death off the 'Troll Wall' in Norway. His 29-year-old compatriot Adam Gibson died jumping in Mexico four months later. They were among 2006's 13 fatalities—the highest annual toll in the sport's history.

BASE jumping requires more skill than sky diving, and very few try it without first acquiring plenty of experience jumping out of planes. The obvious additional difficulty is the very, very short amount of time available if something goes wrong.

Unlike sky divers, BASE jumpers are not leaping into a cushion of wind, but into still air. This makes it harder for the jumper to achieve stability and get the body into the right position to pop the 'chute (because of the short drop time, body positioning is hugely important). Conversely, jumpers cite this lack of turbulence as the beauty of the sport: you feel as if you are really flying, rather than being thrown into a wind tunnel.

Swiss jumper Ueli Gegenschatz argues that BASE jumping is not dangerous if you are meticulous. 'Your life depends on a piece of cloth,' he explains, 'therefore packing is a very decisive moment.' The moment of 'chute or canopy deployment is equally important. The 'pilot' 'chutes are generally carried by hand and as the safe freefall time might be only a couple of seconds, timing is everything. The main canopies tend to be wing-like 'ram air' types. These begin to fly forward as soon as they open, so if you are facing the wrong way, you will be flying straight into a building, antenna, span or earth. The pay-off is that they are highly manoeuvrable, so as long as you respond quickly ram air 'chutes can effectively dodge bits of bridge, support pillars, aerial cables, rock shelves and other things likely to tangle a 'chute—or flatten a jumper.

One of the biggest skills of BASE jumping is to know when to say, 'The conditions aren't right, I'm not going to jump.' This can be hard after having made a very long and difficult climb to the exit point.

Watching a jump starts with the frightening sight of a human falling, usually past rocks, with no obvious protection. But from the other perspective, says BASE jumper Glenn Singleman, it is amazingly serene:

> When you go sky diving, there's a little bit of flying, but it is mostly falling, and you need a smelly noisy aircraft to do it. It is not all that peaceful because there is all this noise and stuff going on.

Your life depends on a piece of cloth, therefore packing is a very decisive moment.

With BASE jumping it is just you with the parachute and the wonderful natural setting you are in. And when you jump off, it is absolutely quiet. When you step off the edge of a cliff it's like the first breath you ever took.

Singleman says it takes a few seconds before the wind really 'starts up':

With sky diving you don't get much of a sense of how fast you are falling. It feels like you are floating on a big bed of wind ... the ground is a distant concept. With BASE jumping you are right near the ground ... You see your acceleration, you see gravity sucking you down towards the ground and you see your speed increasing and you see the cliff, if you look back between your legs, whistling past you. You get this real relativistic appreciation of what you are doing and the environment that you are in.

Singleman, a medical doctor and self-confessed adrenalin junkie, has completed hundreds of jumps and in 2006, with his wife Heather Swan, achieved the highest ever BASE jump. They launched themselves off the 6604-metre Meru Peak in northern India while wearing wingsuits.

Singleman's earlier world-record BASE jump, achieved with Australian Nic Feteris, was a 6258-metre leap off Pakistan's Great Trango Tower in Baltistan in the north of the country in 1992.

One of the quirks of high-altitude parachute jumping is that the low air pressure means the body falls more quickly but the 'chute opens more slowly. Crosswinds can be disastrous. The Great Trango Tower jump was spectacularly captured in the award-winning film *BASEClimb* but Singleman says that for all the clever camera work, no film comes anywhere near capturing the real sensation:

It is the most visceral experience I know of. When you go sky diving or BASE jumping or what we are concentrating on now, wingsuit flying, then you are flying. It's you, it's personal human flight. It is everything you dreamed it would be when you were a kid and you wanted to soar in the clouds and be like a bird.

30

BASEJUMPING

In less than four seconds a BASE jumper can be exceeding 100 kilometres per hour. On a longer jump it can be 'terminal' speed: just under 200 kilometres per hour and as fast as you will go belly-to-the-ground on any full-on sky dive. On a 'terminal' jump, even with everything set up correctly, a BASE jumper experiences a mighty whack when the 'chute opens.

'It is like someone hitting you with a lump of 4x2,' says Singleman. As for the danger aspect, he says 'there are two categories who die ... beginners doing stuff that was too advanced for them, or advanced people pushing their own limits.' But he says the risk is acceptable, first because the right preparation can minimise it and, second, because the challenge of going to the very envelope of human performance and human experience is so worthwhile. Singleman adds:

It's the most visceral experience I know of ... it is everything you dreamed it would be when you were a kid and you wanted to soar in the clouds and be like a bird.

Another of the attractions of rock-climbing, mountaineering and BASE jumping is that you must be present in the moment. There's no thinking about the mortgage or the kids. You are 100 per cent right here right now.

POSSIBLE INJURIES
Multiple fractures, head injuries, paralysis, death.

SOME NOTEWORTHY EXPONENTS

* Carl Boenish. *A well-known American 'freefall cinematographer' whose spectacular footage of the first modern BASE jumpers in the late 1970s helped popularise the new sport. His position as 'the father of BASE jumping' was established in 1981 when he coined the term and began the numbering system. Boenish himself was BASE #4 (his wife Jean was BASE #3). He died in 1984 leaping off the 1100-metre 'Troll Wall' in Norway.*

* Hannes Arch and Ueli Gegenschatz. *This duo of Austrian paraglider/ aerobatics pilot and Swiss sky diver/stuntman made the first jump off the Matterhorn, the highest mountain in the Swiss Alps. The shoulder they jumped from was 4200 metres above sea level, though the sheer drop before they would have hit rocks was just 150 metres. That gave the pair about 2 seconds of freefall and a rather pressing need to steer away from the rock face as soon as their main 'chutes opened.*

* Mat Hoffman. *This American BMXer pioneered BASE riding in 1997, pedalling a bike off a 1000-metre Norwegian cliff, completing a couple of somersaults then pulling a 'chute. He ditched the bike on the way down. Although uninjured on that occasion, in other activities (including world record BMX jumps and riding bikes out of planes) Hoffman has, in his own words, 'had 16 operations, broken over 50 bones, flatlined and been in a coma. It may sound like I'm a bit mental, but it is my passion to push the limits of my mind and body, and to fly into unknown territories and harmonise with them.'*

* Marta Empinotti-Pouchert. *A Brazilian living in the United States, and perhaps the world's most experienced female BASE jumper, with more than 1200 leaps. In 1987 her boyfriend Steve Gyrsting was killed when his 'chute failed to open, but she insisted at the time she 'would die inside' if she had to stop BASE jumping. 'It's always devastating,' Empinotti-Pouchert said in response to a later BASE jumping death. 'But as a jumper, you think, "What's the option?" To live not fully? To be afraid of living? Because people like us—we need this.'*

Heather Swan—
wearing her Vampire
V1 Wingsuit—launches
from Mount Brento, a
1.5-kilometre cliff near
Arco, Italy.

Photo: James Boole
c/- BASEclimb

What's more challenging than BASE jumping? Doing it into a large and dark pothole, of course. This multiple exposure shows Felix Baumgartner disappearing into Mamet Cave, Croatia.

Photo: flohagena.com/Red Bull Photofiles

In 1999 Austrian Felix Baumgartner BASE jumped from the hand of the Christ the Redeemer statue in Rio de Janiero. It was a 38-metre drop he claimed as the world's shortest BASE jump. When Baumgartner later took on the Mamet Cave in Croatia, he was leaping from the daylight of the Velebit National Park into the darkness of a toilet-shaped bowl of jagged rocks. He fell 190 metres, reaching around 170 kilometres per hour before deploying his 'chute just 70 metres from the ground. It opened 20 metres later, giving just 50 metres' margin for terror. Baumgartner used an MP3 player to give him the timing of when to open the chute. His eyes had no chance to adjust to the darkness, robbing him of visual references (other than candles he had organised on the rocky floor), and he needed to steer his purpose-built parachute away from the ground, which sloped away from the hole. The whole thing had taken a huge amount of preparation and involved enormous risks, and had lasted just 7.5 seconds.

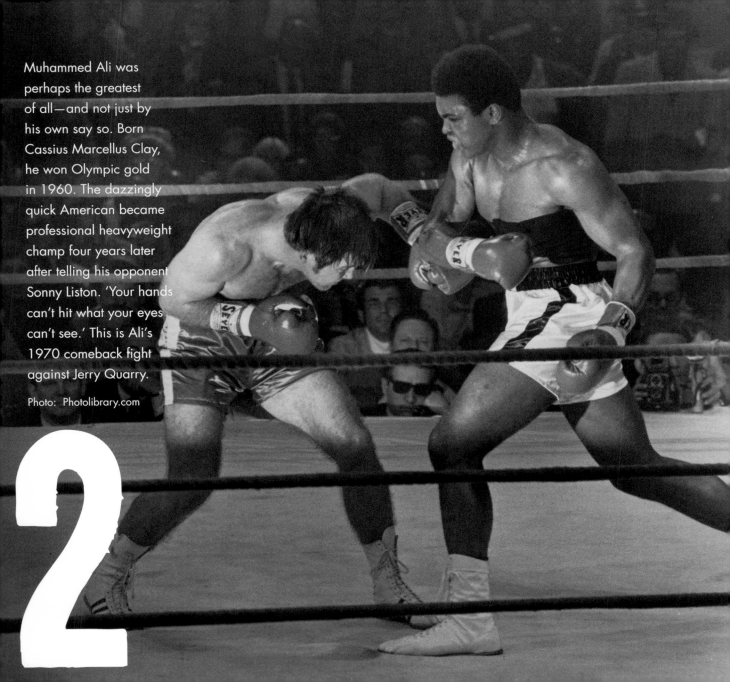

Muhammed Ali was perhaps the greatest of all—and not just by his own say so. Born Cassius Marcellus Clay, he won Olympic gold in 1960. The dazzingly quick American became professional heavyweight champ four years later after telling his opponent Sonny Liston. 'Your hands can't hit what your eyes can't see.' This is Ali's 1970 comeback fight against Jerry Quarry.

Photo: Photolibrary.com

2

BOX
ING

OBJECTIVE

To slam your opponent's brain against the inside of his (or her) skull, in order to induce unconsciousness or incapacity for a count of ten. Failing that, to hit your adversary harder and more often than he or she hits you, and thereby win on points.

REWARDS

International fame. Huge purses for the top fights.

RISKS

Having your brain slammed against the inside of your skull in order to induce unconsciousness—or worse. Becoming punch drunk (i.e., a slobbering old idiot) in later life, with the additional probability of having cauliflower ears, a putty nose and a collection of teeth missing a few of the old favourites.

WHY?

Known by some as the 'sweet science', boxing is the mainstream sport that is closest to true gladiatorial combat (mixed martial arts, or MMA, though more violent, has a much lower profile). As such, boxing is a welcome change from competitive ballroom dancing or synchronised swimming. It can be graceful, too, and involves some of the fittest, strongest athletes in the world. When interviewed in the documentary *When We Were Kings*, writer Norman Mailer pointed out that 'the heavyweight championship produces an excitement in the onlookers that's unlike almost any other spectacle. It's almost physically unendurable to wait for the bell for the first round'.

WHY NOT?

It can be as brutal, primitive and uncivilised as sport gets. While sky divers can complete thousands of jumps without a scratch, every boxer knows he will be injured in pretty well every fight. A line often attributed to the English world middleweight champion Alan Minter—'Sure, there have been injuries and even deaths in boxing, but none of them serious'—is probably apocryphal, though it does seem to say a lot about boxing and boxers. Furthermore, the major heavyweight fights are largely controlled out of places such as Las Vegas by men who look like extras from 'The Sopranos' or *Pulp Fiction*. Things don't always reek of fairness.

THE RUNDOWN

Padded gloves were not introduced to protect boxers' faces. They were brought in to protect their hands and thus allow boxers to hit their opponents harder and more often. They also increase the mass of the fist, causing more damage to the participants' faces—and their brains.

However, many other unsavoury aspects of the sport have been cleaned up considerably since its early origins (boxing appears in artworks dating from at least 1500BC, and was included in the Olympics from 688BC). For example, Roman variations such as wrapping the fighters' hands in leather straps imbedded with sharp metal inserts are now frowned upon.

The modern era of boxing began in England in the seventeenth century, with bare-knuckle prize-fighting. A lack of rules and a lack of any time limit ensured these fights were long, hard and bloody, which was just the way the crowds liked them. It is said that the ring was devised not to keep the boxers in but to keep the brawling spectators out.

Hitting or stamping opponents on the ground, eye-gouging, elbowing, head-butting and much else were all part of the deal, contributing to horrible injuries, frequent deaths—and various legal bans of the sport. Order began to emerge in the eighteenth century and the London 'Prize Ring Rules', arrived in 1838. Quickly adopted in the United States, these stipulated that the fists were the principal weapons, and reduced the number of wrestling techniques allowed.

As boxing became more controlled, its legitimacy grew. So did public interest. It became a favourite sport of the moneyed 'man about town', the first boxing gyms were opened and many began to consider 'pugilism' England's national sport. Boxing terms entered the language—'on the ropes', 'pull your punches' and 'knockout blow' are just a few examples—while 'The Queensberry Rules' (adopted in the 1860s) became a metaphor for fairness and gentlemanly conduct. These rules introduced gloves, three-minute rounds, the '10 count' and weight divisions to boxing.

The nineteenth century saw the sport take off in the United States, and by the twentieth century, America had become the world's number one boxing power. This was partly due to the US Army's adoption of boxing as a training tool, and the subsequent extolling of its masculine virtues by writers such as Jack London and Ernest Hemingway. Increased purses in professional boxing offered a potential escape route from the ghetto, and America's blacks and immigrant classes took to the sport with gusto.

Politics also played its part. Having the world heavyweight champion among your citizens became a strong symbol of national prestige. The 1936 and 1938 fights between the black American, Joe 'Brown Bomber' Louis, and Hitler's paradigm of German racial superiority, Max Schmeling, were famously described as 'the under-card to World War Two'. Muhammad Ali's refusal to fight in Indochina—'No Viet Cong ever called me Nigger,' he is supposed to have said—put a particularly talented and outspoken boxer at the centre of the civil rights and anti-war protest movements.

Since World War Two the most prestigious professional division, the heavyweight, has been dominated by black Americans. Mike Tyson, Evander Holyfield, George Foreman, Joe Frazier, Sonny Liston, Muhammad Ali and others became household names—and at least one of them became a household cooking utensil. Since the 1970s, a small number of women have taken up serious boxing, causing considerable controversy (though, curiously, female boxing was a display sport way back at the 1904 Olympics).

In recent years boxing has been increasingly controlled out of America's gambling states and packaged largely as a bet-fest and pay-per-view TV spectacular. Confusion reigns, with a profusion of governing bodies hosting a plethora of championships, and boxing is demonised around the world as brutal, primitive and unsafe. Yet the sport survives, perhaps precisely because it offers something brutal, primitive and unsafe in a world in which people are increasingly cocooned.

You love the thrill of knocking someone out. Anybody who hasn't knocked anybody out doesn't know that feeling yet.

When you are down on the canvas you don't even know you are down there. You don't know where the punch came from.

In 1987 Joyce Carol Oates wrote that boxing 'is a celebration of the lost art of masculinity,' a notion underscored by many comments from exponents of the 'sweet science'. When touring Australia in 2006, the former world champion Lennox Lewis said, 'Obviously, you love when the crowd cheers for you. You love the thrill of knocking someone out. Anybody who hasn't knocked anybody out doesn't know that feeling yet.'

Joe Bugner sees things slightly differently, he likens boxing to the 'the noble art of self-defence':

If you happen to land a couple of good punches, of course it feels good because you know the fight could end quickly. Your intention is to get rid of this bloke before he gets hurt more.

Anyone who goes in there specifically to try to hurt the guy to the point he might live or die I think is a f_ing moron—please print it like that [we didn't]. They should be banned for life. I have never loved hurting people, it's not in my style.

Joe Bugner is a Hungarian-born fighter who flew first the English and later the Australian flag (as 'Aussie Joe Bugner'). He turned professional at 17 and finally won a world heavyweight championship belt at the grand old age of 48 in 1998. In his younger, more potent days Bugner twice went the distance with Ali.

Under cross examination Bugner does admit that maybe there were one or two times in his 83 pro fights that he did seek to hurt someone:

There was one fighter from Cardiff and his name was Winston Allen and he was ranked number three in Britain and he was a right lunatic so I smashed him and I enjoyed that, but only because he was such a vulgar piece of work.

Like many other fighters, Bugner says the punch that knocks someone out is never the punch you expect to do the worst damage. Likewise, the one that takes you out:

> When you are down on the canvas you don't even know you are down there. You don't know where the punch came from. If you are fit you can recover in a few seconds and get back into it ... as long as you don't get caught with another good punch straight away because then your brain goes whacko and it's like the light goes out:

During the 1930s it was reported that Joe Louis was knocked unconscious by Max Schmeling but stayed on his feet for a whole round and kept punching instinctively. Some have dismissed it as myth, but Bugner insists otherwise:

> It has happened to me. The thumping punch is the one that hurts you. The quick one, you don't even know about that. But when you are being hit hard by a robotic-type fighter, after a while your brain goes into shutdown.

Bugner says when it happens to a fighter you can see that 'foggy, misty look in their eyes' and 'the corner guy has to get ice on to the back of your neck to get the blood flow out of your head area, because when it increases, your brains swells and you've got big problems.'And the worst thing Bugner has seen in the ring?

> When I fought Bonecrusher Smith ... he comes out and hits me with two punches and I thought my head was going to come off my shoulders ... I threw a right hand to his chin and he pulled back about a quarter of an inch and I hit him in the left shoulder. I don't know if you've ever seen a shoulder out of its socket, but I swear to God it was the most grotesque scene I've ever seen. And this man started to scream in the boxing ring. His shoulder was about four inches away from the socket. I didn't know what to say, I didn't know what to do.

Different parts of the brain move at different rates and the overall result is to create a swirling effect inside the brain.

Smith couldn't continue and Bugner won on a TKO, or technical knockout.

POSSIBLE INJURIES

There are almost no injuries that boxers don't suffer in the ring: cuts, bruises, broken bones, dislocated fingers, flat noses and torn ligaments are standard issue. However, anti-boxing campaigns by the British Medical Association (BMA) have concentrated on eye and brain injuries, particularly the latter which are thought to be cumulative. The BMA Working Party Report of 2001 states a direct punch to the head can be likened to being hit by a 12 pound (5.44 kilogram) padded wooden mallet travelling at 20 miles per hour (32 kilometres per hour).

The head rotates sharply and then returns to its normal position at a much slower speed. In addition, the different densities of the different parts of the brain also move at different rates and the overall result is to create a 'swirling' effect inside the brain.

Damage to eyes can include retina detachment or haemorrhage, and even injuries caused by shock waves being generated in the eye's fluid contents.

In 2004 Australia's Danny Green won a fight but suffered such extreme heat stroke he lost his short-term memory and apologised to everyone for being beaten. 'The doctor said I was literally cooking my brain from the inside,' Green later explained. Some believe he was never as good a fighter after that bout. Although hundreds of boxers have suffered fatal injuries in the ring since World War Two, the statistical chances of a boxer dying remain lower than for several other sports, including motor racing and rock fishing.

Jamaican Simon Brown was flattened by a crushing punch from American Vincent Pettway in their 1995 bout, but when Brown hit the deck he continued punching despite being unconscious. Three years later Brown, who didn't consider himself beaten until they had shut the ambulance tailgate, was clouted in the jaw by David Reid. Although unconscious well before his head hit the canvas with a second, equally sickening thud, Brown kept his hands in the defensive position throughout. About 60 seconds later he was revived with an ammonia capsule, his gloves still raised, just in case.

45
BOXING

* Muhammad Ali. *Originally known as Cassius Clay, Ali is often claimed as the world's most famous athlete. He is also the world's most famous victim of Parkinson's Disease, which he insists is not related to having the stuffing bashed out of him in those sad, later fights. At his brilliant best (between 1960 and 1967 by most estimations), Ali floated like a butterfly, stung like a bee and captivated the world with a speed previously unseen in the heavyweight arena. He also had a highly quotable line of chat.*

* Jack Jackson. *The son of former slaves, America's Jackson was the first black world heavyweight champion. He was crowned in 1908, curiously, in Sydney, Australia. The boxing establishment immediately sought to find a white man to beat him. Jackson responded to a torrent of racial abuse by flaunting his wealth and his white girlfriends and by knocking most of his challengers into another space–time continuum. He was eventually jailed under the highly convenient (and variably enforced) Mann Act, like so many other 'uppity' blacks.*

* Jimmy Carruthers. *The first Australian to win a world title, the bantamweight belt in 1952, he did so by spectacularly knocking out the otherwise undefeated South African Vic Towel. Carruthers landed 147 punches to finish the fight in just 139 seconds, and that time included a nine count and a ten count for his opponent. Towel managed just one punch, which missed, before being carted away to hospital.*

* Mike Tyson. *Although he had scarcely enough brains for even a small entrée, the young Tyson had an explosive power that was simply dazzling. In 1986, after becoming the youngest ever heavyweight champion, 20-year-old 'Iron Mike' commenced the most mercurial career trajectory in the history of the sport. He lost and regained championship belts, was jailed for rape, was banned from boxing for various offences inside and outside the ring (famously munching off part of Evander Holyfield's ear during a fight and biting Lennox Lewis's leg during a press conference). He also somehow squandered the tens of millions he earned.*

Knuckle, head: Mike Tyson in his last serious bout. The out-of-form ex-champ gave up at the end of the sixth round against Irish journeyman Kevin McBride. This 2005 fight was a damp squib ending to the most bizarre career in boxing.

Photo: James Squire/Getty Images

Australia's Casey Stoner gets the most out of his machine during qualifying for the 2006 Australian Grand Prix at Phillip Island, Victoria. The top speed in the race exceeded 320 kilometres per hour.

Photo: Australian Grand Prix Corporation

3

MOTO
GP
RACING

OBJECTIVE

To ride an ultra-powerful motorcycle obscenely fast in the hope that you can outpace your opponents without, to quote the late double world champlon Barry Sheene, 'punchin' an 'ole in the scenery'.

50

MOTOGPRACING

REWARDS

For the top riders, international fame and multimillion-dollar salaries. A free supply of attractive and scantily clad women to hold umbrellas over you on the starting grid. Alas though, the riders at the rear of the field face the same dangers but actually pay to be there.

RISKS

'Punchin' an 'ole in the scenery', head-butting a wall, being pole-vaulted onto the bitumen, colliding with other competitors, being run over by other competitors or, during a crash, being king-hit by your own motorcycle.

WHY?

It's the pinnacle of motorcycle road racing: fast, flowing and arguably the most closely competitive motor sport on two wheels or four. Riders banging elbows and knees at 300 kilometres per hour plus is dramatic for spectators and even more so for competitors. The acceleration is simply dazzling and, for any aficionado, the sound of a racing engine at full roar beats any symphony. Claudio Costa, doctor of philosophy as well as medicine, is famous for patching up the elite motorcycle riders and getting them back on track in record time. In the documentary *Faster* he explains why it is worth the risk and pain:

> In the rider's veins there are drops of Dionysian madness which are beautiful because they give the heroes of motorcycling the power to live life fully.

MotoGP racing also leads to the development of useful road bike technology.

WHY NOT?

It's phenomenally noisy and stupidly expensive, with variations in equipment quality often masking or flattering the efforts of the riders.

THE RUNDOWN

At first glance you think these guys are nuts, the second one pretty well confirms it. MotoGP has had different names through the years and has been run to different regulations but, essentially, it is the premier class of motorcycle road racing and attracts the world's bravest, fastest and, occasionally, most foolhardy riders. They compete in a multi-round championship made up of national Grand Prix races.

Until 2002 the bikes were known as '500s' and powered by half-litre two-stroke engines. After that the machines were powered by 990cc four-stroke engines then, from the 2007 season, 800cc four-strokes. They produce about twice the power of a typical four-cylinder hatchback—yet weigh only an eighth as much. Speeds have exceeded 340 kilometres per hour.

Because motorcycles are narrow and nimble, they can race four and five abreast. The riders steer by leaning, in the process achieving angles that seem to defy physics and rubbing their feet, knees and elbows on the ground. During acceleration the front wheel often lifts off the ground. While braking the tail can rise well clear of the road, severely reducing grip, stability and, sometimes, longevity. In heavy cornering the riders are often sliding the front and rear wheels; at all points they are relying on tyre contact areas about the size of a human hand to keep them from disaster. Multiple lead changes on each lap are common.

Mentally, the sport is draining because it is necessary to maintain phenomenal concentration levels for three-quarters of an hour. And letting a machine push you around is physically harder than you might imagine, particularly when it comes to making the bike continually change direction at high speed. This requires fighting the gyroscopic effect of the spinning wheels, which wants to keep the bike upright.

Top-level riders tend to cut casts off broken limbs after two and three weeks so they can keep racing. Very few last at the top much into their thirties because their bodies can no longer recover from injury quickly enough to stay competitive. They may be brave but they are not fearless.

'There's fear, there's always fear, but you need that fear to prepare yourself physically and mentally,' says 1987 world champ Wayne Gardner. 'That apprehension heightens your skills, too. It is the flirt with danger that makes it exciting, the vulnerability.'

This vulnerability has increased at a much faster rate than rider protection, while Formula One cars, by comparison, have been made remarkably safe.

'I have a very competitive streak in me, want to push the limits in everything and riding motorcycles is good fun,' says Gardner:

> I've raced many a car but you are just strapped in … it is a bit like going to the dentist, you don't bond a relationship with the vehicle. On a motorbike you and the bike become one. Racing a car is a more clinical affair. In a car you can't fall over. A bike even sitting on its stand can fall over. You've got all these axis changes when you are riding it, left or right, forward or back, yaw forward and back, left and right.

Gardner says that after a victory he would be walking on air for a week—'the adulation straight after the race is great.' When he didn't win, well, 'There were days of black moods. I'd be personally crucifying myself to work out why I hadn't won.'

And what is a crash like?

> It all happens really quickly but at a certain point it slows down and as you are going over you are thinking 'this is going to hurt, this is going to hurt'. That's when the slow motion kicks in, in a way you can see the whole thing happening in slow motion, you can see yourself going over the bike, see yourself about to hit the ground.

In the rider's veins there are drops of Dionysian madness … they give the heroes of motorcycling the power to live life fully.

53
MOTO GP RACING

There's fear, there's always fear, but you need that fear to prepare yourself physically and mentally. It is the flirt with danger that makes it exciting, the vulnerability.

You tend to look around and see if there are any bikes about to hit you, if you are away from your own bike and then you are just waiting ... waiting ... waiting ... for the train to hit you. Then you kind of go limp, you kind of have a moment of sudden black-out, depending on how hard you hit the ground.

The initial impact is like someone has given you this almighty uppercut in the back or the stomach. It takes your breath away. Then you are trying to get presence of mind to work out where your bike is around you and where you are heading. When bones break you can feel it immediately. It's a bit like when you take a full packet of crisps and just crush them. That's the noise and sensation and it goes right through your body:

Gardner insists sliding along the ground doesn't hurt, even at 200 kilometres per hour or more.

Sometimes when you are sliding along and it starts to get a bit warm in one spot, you can roll over or change your position to share it around. You are more interested in if there any walls, any ditches coming up. Then when you stop, you start working out whether you can move everything. My initial thing is 'I've got to get up'. The adrenalin kills the pain, but you know there's a major problem if, for example, your leg is facing the other way.

And when things are going well? 'Nothing beats that feeling of freedom, nothing.'

POSSIBLE INJURIES

The serial breaking of bones comes with the territory. Severe head and spinal injuries are also strong possibilities, though, statistically, death is rare (that being said, Daijiro Kato died in 2003, after smashing at the Suzuka circuit in Japan). Many riders have had fingers, or parts thereof, ground off after trapping them under sliding motorcycles. The crash that ended Mick Doohan's career came in qualifying for the Spanish Grand Prix in Jerez 1999, when he came off at 200 kilometres per hour, hitting a sand trap then a concrete wall. He later explained: 'I broke my leg into about 17 pieces, my foot, my hand, my arm, shoulders, ribs, just a couple of little odds and ends.'

Doohan's one-time team-mate Darryl Beattie rolled his Honda Grand Prix bike and caught his left foot in the chain. It was dragged through the rear sprocket, pureeing all five toes.

Line astern: Italy's multiple motorcycle world champions Max Biaggi and Valentino Rossi in a tight MotoGP pack at the 2001 AGP at Phillip Island.

Photo: Australian Grand Prix Corporation

Two tyres sliding, eyes
almost certainly open
very widely indeed.
Gardner en route
to his 1987 world
championship.

Photo: Honda Australia

In the 1990 US Grand Prix at Laguna Seca, Eddie Lawson broke his heel bone into six pieces, one of which was described by doctors as 'completely crushed'. Randy Mamola dislocated bones in his wrist, Australia's Wayne Gardner badly damaged his ankle and compatriot Kevin McGee was flung against the tarmac and left in a coma. Kevin Schwantz was fighting for the lead towards the end of the race when he crashed and was thrown off his bike at a turn evocatively known as '11'. The Texan rider jumped back up and grabbed the handlebars, only to watch his left arm collapse between the elbow and wrist, as if the bones had been replaced by old rope. He was unable to continue, not least because he couldn't engage the clutch. Despite the severity of the injury, Schwantz refused to have it 'pinned', went jet-skiing a few days later with his arm in a plastic bag and then had it strapped in a 'racing position' so he could compete in the next Grand Prix.

SOME NOTEWORTHY EXPONENTS

* **Mick Doohan.** He became a five-time world champion (1994 to 1998) in the premier category, but in his first season the young Australian was christened by the press gallery 'Dead by June Doohan'. He tried to live up to it by regularly Liverpool kissing the bitumen, smacking himself against concrete walls and single-handedly causing a staffing crisis in the emergency department nearest each track. Nonetheless, Doohan had sublime ability and unrivalled focus and, once he learned to stay upright on a Grand Prix bike, he was almost unbeatable. He was famously dour on race weekends—he later admitted it was to make sure his rivals didn't have a clue what he was thinking. 'I don't know where I get the determination from,' he once said, 'I just hate losing.'

* **Valentino Rossi.** A flamboyant and extravagantly gifted Italian rider who won titles in the 125cc and 250cc classes before moving into the premier class and winning five consecutive titles (2001 to 2005). Rossi still has some way to go to catch fellow Italian Giacomo Agostini, who won 15 world titles in a variety of categories between 1966 and 1975, but Rossi is also a dab hand in a rally car and was courted by Ferrari for Formula One. He decided to stay on two wheels.

* **Barry Sheene.** This British star of the 1970s was colourful and verbose in several languages and the complete opposite of today's typical health-obsessed, early-to-bed riders. He smoked and drank heavily and often raced after a huge night out. Yet he still won two world championships. Sheene also had several monstrous crashes and retired to Australia's Gold Coast in the hope that the collection of 30 metal plates, pins and screws holding his bones together would cause him less bother in warmer weather.

* **Wayne Rainey.** A brilliant American rider who won three consecutive world titles (1990 to 92) while escaping almost all the usual injuries. That was until his guardian angel bundied off early one afternoon in Italy in 1993 and a relatively unspectacular 'off' left Rainey paraplegic. He went on to race a hand-controlled vehicle in the world SuperKart series.

Wayne Gardner hammering it at Jarama, Spain, in 1987. The Australian rider went on to win the race and the world championship.

Photo: Honda Australia

Dicing with breath:
Tanya Streeter
ascending after another
record-breaking free
diving feat. She opted
for separate flippers
rather than a 'monofin'.

Photo: Lawrence Curtis

4

FREE
DIVING

OBJECTIVE

To descend into bodies of water as deeply as possible or for as long as possible, with no artificial breathing apparatus. And, hopefully, to come up the same number of times as you go down.

REWARDS

The locales are usually very scenic and many free divers report euphoria at great depths. Financially speaking, though, rewards are pretty slim. Patrons are not easy to find, though makers of underwater watches and other related products occasionally kick in. Spectators are also a bit thin on the ground, which is doubly difficult since the action is under the water.

RISKS

Sleeping with the fishes. As depth increases and body chemicals change, divers can lose consciousness without warning, inhale water involuntarily and sink back into the deep.

WHY?

Diving deep under the water without scuba gear places humans in such a harsh environment that the body completely changes the way it works and reveals abilities hitherto unknown. Some free divers believe these abilities demonstrate our closeness to aquatic mammals such as whales and dolphins. Champion Italian Umberto Pelizzari has argued that free diving can provide a mystical experience bordering on the divine:

> *From the depth of 100 metres and more, headlong in the abyss, the heartbeat gets slower, the body disappears, and all the feelings take a new form. The only thing that remains in us is the soul ... Deep down, I am immensely alone but inside it feels as if all humanity is with me ... It is here that I become one with the sea and discover my true self.*

You probably have to be there, but others have reported remarkably similar sensations.

WHY NOT?

It's a submersive activity. Ultra-deep diving is akin to playing Russian Roulette according to some critics, who also argue it has very little to do with sport or athletic endeavour. When you discover you've exceeded your abilities, you can be a long way from the surface. And multiple world-record breaker Tanya Streeter says it's not always elegant: 'You have to spit in your mask, you have snot coming out your nose, then there's the sunburn. The mask lines are the worst; they stick around for about six hours afterwards.'

THE RUNDOWN

The modern sport of free diving, or competitive apnea, is split into various categories. One is 'static apnea', or holding your breath while staying still. Germany's Tom Sietas, for example, has remained beneath the water for nine minutes. Amazing, but also amazingly dull to watch.

Another is 'dynamic apnea', where Sietas again excels. On a single breath he can swim 183 metres under the water of an Olympic pool, without fins (and without surfacing). Add fins and he can cover 223 metres.

However, it is when free divers aim for maximum depth that the sport moves from 'interesting' to 'extreme and fascinating'. The body comes under extraordinary pressure from the weight of the water and an extreme mammalian diving reflex kicks in.

This reflex is some sort of strange genetic memory, buried in our wiring from the days when our protoplasmic forebears were still considering whether to stay in the primeval slime, or climb out and invent bungee jumping and flat-screen televisions. As the diving depth increases, the heart rate decreases dramatically and the circulation completely changes. There is peripheral vasoconstriction, that is, the extremities are deprived of blood (and the oxygen it carries) so it can instead be sent to the heart and brain. The spleen contracts and releases oxygen-rich red blood cells. Blood also rushes in to support the lungs and ribcage, which would otherwise collapse. The same reflex is present in penguins, whales, seals and dolphins.

'Free' diving goes back a long way, though it wasn't usually done for recreation. Young men from the Greek islands risked their lives to support their families by pulling sponges off the ocean floor. In Broome, Western Australia, and Bahrain in the Perisan Gulf divers weighed themselves down with stones to dive for pearls, often descending 30 metres over and over again in a day's work. And often killing themselves well before their time.

Since the late 1950s there has been a vogue for competitive sea diving in Europe, with a special focus on outright depth. The simplest form of modern deep-water free diving is Constant Weight. The diver must descend from the water's surface with no assistance, reach the maximum depth he or she can, and make it back to the top without blacking out or suffering a 'samba' (the ironic term used when a diver reaches the surface but immediately goes into convulsions). Both are big dangers, though free divers consider them just part of the job. Anything taken down in Constant Weight must be hauled back to the surface. There are 'with fins' and 'without fins' categories, with the respective record depths a remarkable 111 metres and 80 metres.

Often these deep-water divers have both feet pushed into a huge, stiff 'monofin'. One of the many difficulties is that the huge exertion of swimming down to such depths uses a large amount of the air the diver needs to ward off hypoxia (or oxygen starvation).

The Variable Weight category sees the diver use a weighted 'sled' to achieve the desired depth, then leave it behind to make his or her way back to the surface. Pulling on a rope is allowable during ascent.

The No Limit category is, as the name implies, the most extreme. The diver uses a weighted sled to go as deep as possible, dropping into the drink at more than 3 metres a second. Flotation balloons and other devices can be used to get back up.

The deeper you go the more 'narced' you are so it is harder to focus. You need to automate everything so it is not a thinking process.

I have found what I call the seventh sense where you can feel every cell living like an individual. You are not one person you are billions of persons. You feel pure joy ...

Ultra-deep diving was made world famous and glamorous by Frenchman Luc Besson's 1988 film *Le Grand Bleu* (*The Big Blue*). An estimate widely published—and equally widely unsourced—claims that in the year after the film's release 500 people around the world died trying to emulate the feats depicted in the film.

Apnea contestants need to equalise the middle ear pressure to that of the surrounding sea to prevent their eardrums from collapsing; the most radical of them flood their sinuses and middle ear with sea water. It is said that many Greek sponge divers just 'broke' their eardrums to avoid the hassle.

At great depths, the pressure on organs with air spaces increases dramatically. Lungs are squeezed to the size of tennis balls, and hypoxia can cause you to pass out without warning. Furthermore, 'nitrogen narcosis', the drunk-like symptoms sometimes known as 'the rapture of the deep', can impair your judgement and reduce your focus at critical moments. Carbon dioxide pressure in your blood (nature's warning system to breathe) can build up to the point where inhaling is involuntary. Drowning can quickly follow, hence the presence of safety divers in properly organised competitions and record attempts.

The first free diving world championship was held in 1996 by the sanctioning body AIDA (the International Association for Development of Apnea). In 2006 Austrian airline pilot Herbert Nitsch set both a Constant Weight record (111 metres) and the official No Limit record (183 metres). So what happens when you plunge to such profundity?

The deeper you go the more 'narced' you are so it is harder to focus. You need to automate everything so it is more like a reaction and not a thinking process.

Nitsch is motivated by 'the kicks and the results'. He says if he has equalised properly, he doesn't feel any pain from the water pressure:

You can't really feel that much the blood shift either. I try to induce it before the dive by doing negative dives. I exhale, go upside down in the water and pump all the air out that I have in my lungs until nothing comes out any more and just with the last mouth fill I go down to 10 metres ...

At the bottom I suck the diaphragm up to give even more negative pressure, basically to induce the blood shift before the dive, which is reducing the residual volume [the air that remains in the lungs even after a maximum exhalation]. I feel I am a bit heavier in the water. And also it reduces the urge to breathe.

It doesn't sound like fun:

No, the preparation is not the fun part of the dive. The actual dive can be fun. No, enjoyable I would put it.

Nitsch says he has achieved 200 metres 'more or less' in practice dives and is planning a '700 feet' (that's about 213 metres) world-record attempt. Record attempts are performed in warm water as fighting the cold wastes energy and therefore oxygen. Even thinking wastes oxygen, though Tanya Streeter says 'what we do as free divers is find the most efficient way of using as little oxygen as possible. The brain does get pretty damn fuzzy ... and the benefit of focusing outweighs what little oxygen it might use.'

According to a study by Eric Seedhouse from the Extreme Physiology Program at Simon Fraser University, Canada, some competitors have recorded a heart rate of just eight or nine beats a minute at the bottom of their dives.

Patrick Musimu, a Belgian, says every time he dives very deeply he finds enlightenment. It happens beyond the 160-metre mark when, as he puts it, his body disappears:

> The body ceases to send me some feedback, and there is a complete disassociation … [here] the intellectual and the spiritual entities start coming out. It is like I am watching myself going inside and outside of my body and for me it is pure magic. People ask me was I afraid and I say I can't be afraid.
>
> I have found what I call the seventh sense where you can feel every cell living like an individual. You are not one person you are billions of persons. All these cells can feel. You feel pure joy …

Doesn't that sound like nitrogen narcosis?

'I say it could be', says Musimu, 'but you haven't seen what I have seen and felt what I have felt. I was touching the sky down there.'

POSSIBLE INJURIES

Brain damage from oxygen depletion, general hypoxia causing unconsciousness, seizure, coma or death. Extreme pain from middle ear, sinus or lung barotraumas. Tanya Streeter argues that although there are risks, they are entirely controllable. 'The safety divers are at much bigger risk, breathing at 400 feet [122 metres], than I am holding my breath.'

Nonetheless, 36-year-old Frenchman Loïc Leferme—one time holder of the No Limit world record—added to the free diving fatality list in April 2007. Leferme, who was training to regain the No Limit crown from Herbert Nitsch, descended to 171 metres off the south coast of France, but an equipment problem slowed the return journey. He blacked out 18 metres from the surface and couldn't be revived.

Jacques Mayol. The real-life diving rivalry between Frenchman Jacques Mayol and the Italian Enzo Maiorca was the inspiration for the film **The Big Blue**. Mayol himself was one of the scriptwriters. He believed that man had extraordinary aquatic abilities that could be unlocked by training. 'One day babies of the future will be reconnected to the aquatic evolutionary past. They will be totally in harmony with the sea and diving and playing at great depth with their marine cousins, holding the breath for a long period of time and giving birth in the sea even in the presence of dolphins. Homo Delphinus is not just a concept.' Mayol proved it to some extent by becoming the first person to free dive to 100 metres. Suffering from depression, he hanged himself in 2001 but not before predicting that man would one day dive to 200 metres and hold his breath for 10 minutes.

* **Umberto Pelizzari.** An Italian who boasts a lung volume of 7.9 litres, about a third more than average. (Cyclist Lance Armstrong has 7 litres, and English rower Peter Reed's 9.38 litres is thought to be the highest recorded.) Pelizzari was a major force in the development of modern free diving. He set 17 world records, then quit competition to dive for pleasure.

* **Tanya Streeter.** Born in the Cayman Islands, schooled in Britain and now living in Texas, Streeter achieved a depth of 122 metres in 2003 in the Variable Weight category, beating both the male and female records. It is extremely rare in any sport for a female athlete to hold an open record, but the remarkable Streeter has done it several times, including a depth of 160 metres in the No Limit category in 2002. Unlike some, she doesn't flood her air cavities: 'I think it increases your risk of succumbing to narcosis and oxygen toxicity, purely because if you do it you can descend so much faster, to crazy, crazy depths and expose yourself to more dangers. I see it as unnatural. There aren't many other mammals that flood their cavities and I believe we are marine mammals.'

* **Patrick Musimu.** In an unratified (but filmed) dive in 2005 this 36-year-old Belgian diving champion and kick-boxer reached the extraordinary depth of 209.6 metres. 'Experts did calculations and said my body wouldn't adapt to the pressure,' Musimu explained. 'They said my lungs would collapse, or my trachea would collapse at around 180 metres. They said the blood would come out, the negative pressure will suck it out into my lungs and trachea and destroy everything, tissue will tear. I just had this vision that I could do it ... I knew there were obstacles but I thought they were mainly in people's minds.' The dive took 3 minutes 28 seconds from start to finish. Musimu believes we will see dives of 240 or

TRULY MAD MOMENTS

The one event that has brought free diving the most notoriety was the death of 28-year-old Frenchwoman Audrey Mestre. It was in waters near the Dominican Republic in 2002 that Mestre, a glamorous former marine biology student, stood on a weighted sled, took a very deep breath and was dropped down to 171 metres beneath the sea. That's the height of a 50-storey building. Mestre was taking part in a No Limit record attempt organised by her husband, the legendary Cuban diver Francisco Ferraras, better known as 'Pipín'. As well as being a talented free diver, Pipín is something of a fantasist; his autobiography claims that as a teenager, he was swimming so deeply off the coast of Cuba that he was picked up on the sonar of a Soviet submarine, which raised an alarm that called in the Cuban Navy to investigate. The record Mestre was trying to beat was Pipín's own, but on arriving at the bottom of her run Mestre discovered that the balloon supposed to lift her back to the surface wouldn't inflate. What's more, two of the rescue divers weren't where they were supposed to be. The entire dive was to take 3 minutes but Mestre was under for 8 minutes 48 seconds. When she was brought to the surface, there was no possibility of resuscitation. Her story is slated to be the subject of a film directed by *Titanic*'s James Cameron, himself a keen diver.

'I believe we are marine mammals,' says free diver Tanya Streeter. Here she is at Turks and Caicos Island, USA, in 2003—a year in which she broke various male and female world records.

Photo: Paul Streeter/Red Bull Photofiles

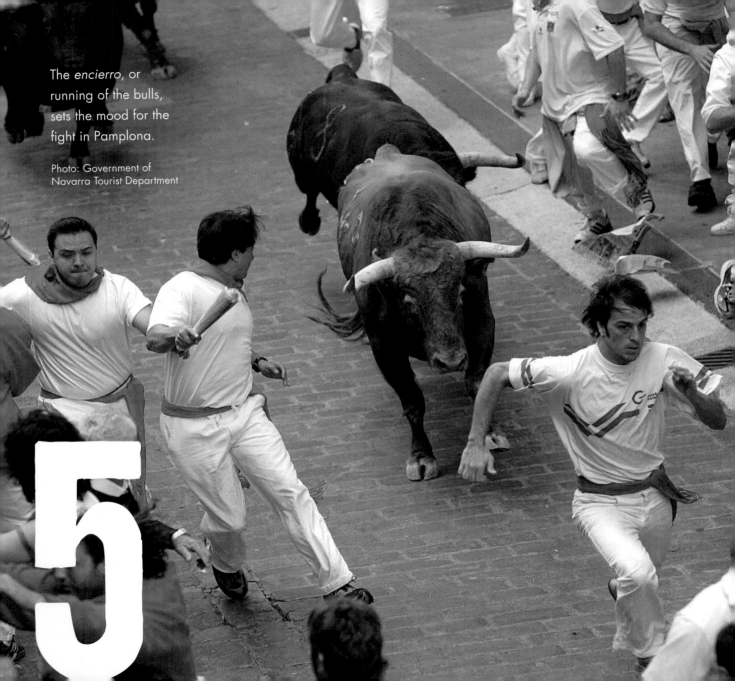

The *encierro*, or running of the bulls, sets the mood for the fight in Pamplona.

Photo: Government of Navarra Tourist Department

5

BULL
FIGHT
ING

OBJECTIVE

To taunt a large and aggressive animal with horns, and eventually kill it by plunging a sword between its shoulder blades, all while wearing very tight trousers and a sparkly jacket.

REWARDS

Top competitors receive enormous pay-packets and get the pop star treatment, though only in a limited number of countries (mainly Spain and its former colonies). Newcomers pay to compete. The most revered matadors are celebrated in songs, movies and books and, in the 1950s and 1960s, many of them got to sleep with Ava Gardner. There are children's toys and decorative plates made in the likeness of famous matadors. The bulls do well only very occasionally; in 1879 'Murcielago' demonstrated such courage in the ring he was pardoned and then mated with 70 cows, in the hope his children would be as feisty as he was. He also had a Lamborghini named after him, though posthumously (and probably not available in his size and preferred colour).

RISKS

Having a large and aggressive animal with horns misunderstand the objective of the exercise and kill you instead. Spain's fighting bulls are the most belligerent known to man and need no fancy red capes waved in their face to attack. Even if a matador escapes complete evisceration in his career, he will almost certainly at various times be battered, trampled, thrown and gored (one medical text describes goring as a difficult-to-treat mix of a wound, burn, contusion and infection. To put it another way, yuk.). There is also a newer hazard: threatening text messages and even letter bombs from animal rights activists.

WHY?

It's not only opponents of bull fighting who argue that it isn't a sport. The greatest supporters of the *corrida de toros* believe it is something even more elevated: an art-form akin to dynamic sculpture. In his famous tome on the subject, *Death in the Afternoon*, Ernest Hemingway wrote it was 'the only art in which the artist is in danger of death,' though it should be said he didn't live to see freestyle sky diving, or various other modern blendings of art and sport. However you classify bull fighting, it is impossible to deny the huge enthusiasm it engenders in Latin countries. Apparently the bulls love it, too. As Cristina Sànchez, one of the few successful matadoras, once said, 'They are brave, born to die in the ring and help create an act of art with a person.'

WHY NOT?

It's cruel, brutal and playing to bloodlust, irrespective of whether the spectators are waiting to see the matador or the bull die. It is the only stadium sport where the specific aim is to kill, and it goes further: it sets out to make an elaborate, choreographed spectacle of death. Accusations of corruption are never far away, including stories of bulls being nobbled by such techniques as drugging or spraying oil into their eyes. According to Cecilio Paniagua, MD, writing in *The Psychoanalytic Quarterly*, 'the central appeal of bull fighting is sadistic gratification, which seems to be of a mostly parricidal nature.' So there.

THE RUNDOWN

An eleventh-century Castilian military leader named Rodrigo Díaz de Vivar (otherwise known as El Cid and played by gun-nut Charlton Heston in the 1961 Hollywood epic) is often credited with first lancing a bull from horseback. It was a bad day for Spanish bulls, and things never really improved. El Cid's action supposedly set off a craze for killing bulls among the influential and well-to-do in the Iberian peninsula, which in turn led to the modern form of the corrida de toros.

Spain now has over 300 bull rings and many ranches dedicated to breeding good toros—the mark of a good toro being its fierceness toward the young men who step in the ring with it.

Like any other piece of theatre, a Spanish bull fight is conducted in acts. The major part of the first act, or tercio, involves two or three picadors on horseback. They use picas (spears) to stab the bull at the base of the neck when it instinctively charges their horses. This is meant to test the bull's courage but it also serves to weaken its neck muscles and make it harder to raise its head for a more accurate charge. Since 1930 the picadors' horses have been protected by body armour; before that they were gored frequently and known to trip over their own entrails as they tried to flee.

The second tercio plays out with banderilleros waving capes at the bull and placing staves or barbed darts in its back. Again this is to keep the bull 'lively'—and why wouldn't it?—but further reduces its ability to fight. It also keeps the bull's head lower, assisting the matador when it is time to plunge the sword.

The final tercio belongs to the star attraction, the matador. Squeezed into his suit of lights (a fetching little silk jacket-and-pants set heavily embroidered in gold and silver beading), the matador will have already appeared for a few passes in acts one and two, carrying his capote, or big work cape. He is now at the business end of his performance, hence the alternate term for the third act—'the moment of truth'.

The matador must now 'play' with the bull, drawing its horns dangerously close his body with his muleta (a much smaller cape than the capote) in a series of complex and graceful passes intended to wear the bull out. The matador's final act is to reach over the horns and push his *estoque* or sword down to the hilt between the bull's shoulder blades. If he gets the strike right the blade should severe the aorta and the bull should die quickly. If a matador does well on the day, the judge may award him an ear (excellent work), two ears (a gold star and two ticks) or two ears plus the tail (go to the top of the class).

Each of the matador's different moves has a name and bull fighting's vocabulary runs to hundreds of unique words. The journalists who cover it are not considered to be sports writers but critics; their reports appear in the Arts pages.

They may dress like ponces and often be obsessive on the hair care front, but matadors are as tough as they are well-groomed. In Seville in 2005, 22-year-

It's a spectacle, a form of entertainment ... it is the slaughtering of a bull in public with an artistic element.

77

BULLFIGHTING

old Sebastian Castella was gored clean through the thigh but still managed to kill the bull. Not only that, half an hour later, he killed a second one. Castella spent the time in between the two fights refusing any medical treatment and bandaging his own wound, which included a severed sciatic nerve. He was gored twice more that season.

The only Englishman to achieve the rank of senior matador is Frank Evans, who retired in 2005. A colourful former butcher from Lancashire, Evans survived 175 fights and was taken to heart by the Spanish as 'El Ingles'. Rather than being lauded by his countrymen, however, he was usually treated as a figure of fun. The media pointed out (correctly) that he trained in a suburban park, using a shopping trolley equipped with horns. He didn't help his own campaign to be taken seriously when he was flattened and trampled by a bull during a fight on the Costa Del Sol. Evans dusted himself down and told the press, 'The f_ing wife hits me harder than that.'

When asked about 'the sport', Evans says:

> It is not a sport at all, because by definition a sport means you have two sides on paper both fairly equal and the outcome is in doubt.
>
> When you look at bull fighting the sides are totally unequal. The man is more intelligent. The bull doesn't have the same intelligence but has vastly more strength and power. Also the outcome is not in doubt.
>
> It's a spectacle, a form of entertainment ... It is the slaughtering of a bull in public with an artistic element.

For Evans, 'it's a tremendous thrill and a tremendous ego trip and so you do risk your life to do it.' He believes reflexes and courage are the most important things for a bull fighter—along with personality:

> We all do the same thing, for example we all make a right-handed pass and the mechanics of the pass are the same for everybody, to get a bull past you, to link passes. So what is the difference? Why is one fellow more artistic than another?

The difference is your personality.

It's a mixture of science and art in a funny way, because at all times you have to employ the correct technique otherwise you are not going to get away with it, but all that you do has to be done with quality and timing. Bull fighters are required to do it with your hips forward and your chest sticking out. It sounds unusual to say that, and to do it when there is no bull there is a simple thing. When you have a bull threatening your life it takes on a certain emotion because you are doing it in the face of danger.

The biggest challenge for everyone is the kill ... It is the first time in the bull fight that you take your eyes off the horns.

Evans accepts that injury from some 'nasty cattle' is an inevitable part of the profession:

You survive because you are very fit by nature of the activity and the training you do.

And what does it feel like to be gored? 'It's very quick, it doesn't hurt. The whole thing is a pretty painless experience really. The pain is afterwards ... after you wake up after surgery.'

Bizarrely, greatly improved medical treatment has enabled matadors to get more hurt more often. Using many of the accelerated techniques developed to help smashed-up motorcycle racers 'get back on track', doctors have taken matadors with gorings that would have been fatal only a generation or two ago, patched them up and enabled them to return to the ring within weeks. This improved chance of survival has encouraged many matadors to take greater risks.

I was gored in the back, in the arse, in 1984 here in Spain. I was gored in 1967 in France and I got another nasty one in 2004 in Mexico.

It may send animal rights people incandescent, but there is nothing marginal about bull fighting in Spain. There are nearly 40 000 individual bull fights a year (very few of which are won by bulls) and by one estimate the industry employs more than 1 per cent of the Spanish workforce. It will take more than Chrissie Hynde and a few placard-wavers to stop it.

POSSIBLE INJURIES

A ten-year Mexican study (Rudloff, Gonzalez, Fernandez, et al. 1994–2004) reported that:

> In all, 68 out of 750 bullfighters (9.06 per cent) required emergency assistance during bullfighting. Trauma to the upper and lower extremity was most common (66 per cent), followed by injuries to the inguinal (8 per cent) and perineal area (7 per cent). Extremity injuries included penetrating wounds requiring operative debridement in 64 per cent of cases, articular dislocations in 4 per cent, closed fractures in 4 per cent, and open fractures in 1 per cent of cases. Major vascular injuries occurred in 5 per cent of the cases. Penetrating inguinal and penetrating perineal injuries were associated with major vascular injuries to the femoral vessels, necessitating operative repair in 33 per cent of the cases.

You get the picture. In short, the chances of getting hurt are very high. If it isn't torn flesh or punctured organs, it could be a broken neck or head injuries, after being tossed by a bull and spearing the ground head-first.

Coats of many colours: pageantry and tradition remain major components in bull fighting—as does the regular goring of matadors. But don't be misled by cerise boots or floral jackets: bullfighters are as tough as any other athletes (or, by their own say so, any other artists).

Photo: Government of Navarra Tourist Department

Running scared: the *encierro* in Pamplona.

Photo: Alamy stock photography

Audience participation is a big thing in bull fighting. Young men are known to leap illegally into the ring during a fight and 'have a go'. Sometimes they die, sometimes they launch brilliant careers (it was as a fence-jumping *espontáneo* that 'El Cordobés' started his career). The ultimate in audience participation, though, happens before the fight. The *encierro,* or running of the bulls, happens off-piste, when the fighting bulls are herded through the streets to the ring in preparation for the afternoon's fights. Hundreds and even thousands of adrenalin-filled men (and the occasional woman) don white shirts and red scarfs and run with them. They taunt the bulls, rub against them and risk goring, trampling and anything else that can be done to a human by an even-toed ungulate the size of a Holden Barina. The most famous *encierro* is held in the northern Spanish city of Pamplona, and the event is now further spiced up by the addition of large numbers of drunk foreigners. Each morning during the Festival of San Fermin a rocket is fired at 8 a.m. and the bulls and the runners take to the 850-metre route in a three-minute blast of colour, movement and, often, harm. There have been at least 14 deaths since the 1920s; in 2003 alone there were 57 serious injuries, including 11 gorings—one of which pierced the bladder and colon of a 27-year-old American.

83
BULLFIGHTING

* **Juan Belmonte.** *The most famous bull fighter of the early twentieth century. In the course of killing 1650 bulls, Belmonte (1892 to 1962) revolutionised the sport by working much closer to the bull's horns than anyone had previously. Ernest Hemingway praised the Spaniard's cojones and, in* **Death in the Afternoon**, *said Belmonte would 'wind a bull around him like a belt'. The technique contributed to him being shockingly injured many times but he survived until old age, which he spent breeding fighting bulls to gore a whole new generation. Belmonte fatally shot himself in the head a year after Hemingway, his friend, did likewise.*

* **Vincent Hitchcock.** *The first English matador, a posh-speaking, swashbuckling, Boy's Own adventurer, who fought bulls in the 1940s and 1950s. Hitchcock never reached great heights in bull fighting but his book* **A Suit of Light** *inspired Frank Evans and others. A Brit calling himself Henry Higgins (strictly speaking, he was the Colombian-born offspring of an English father and Mexican mother) was managed for a short while in the 1960s by Brian Epstein, of Beatles fame. Higgins had a short career, however, and was eventually killed in a hang gliding accident. Other foreign fighters include several Americans (most famously, Sydney Franklin). Atsuhiro Shimoyama, a Japanese matador known as 'Niño Del Sol Naciente' ('The kid from the rising sun'), ended up in a wheelchair. An Australian named Al Brown impressed crowds with his bravery in the 1950s but his short career ended when he was gored in the stomach in Valencia.*

* **Manuel Benítez Pérez.** *Otherwise known as 'El Cordobés', Pérez was the most famous matador of the 1960s. In August 1965, he managed to kill 64 bulls, and in that season he fought in a record 111 corridas (beating the record set by Juan Belmonte). 'El Cordobés' managed to make retirement age despite such unwise habits as kissing bulls between their horns, and advancing towards them with his back turned.*

* **Julian Lopez Escobar.** *'El Juli' made his name in Mexico in the 1990s because he was too young to compete in his native Spain. By the age of 17 he was back in Europe, had become the highest-paid matador of all time, and had already been seriously ventilated four times by enraged bulls. More gorings followed, as did more adulation. As we went to press, he was still receiving ears and tails at the grand old age of 24.*

English senior bullfighter Frank Evans overrun by a less than happy bull. The man known to Spaniards as 'El Ingles' told the press his wife hit him harder.

Photo: Alamy stock photography

Maybe wearing silver pants helped, but with this amazing jump in Planica, Slovenia, Andreas Goldberger covered 225 metres—the year was 2000 and it was a new world ski flying record.

Photo: Calle Törnström/Red Bull Photofiles

6

88
SKI JUMPING

OBJECTIVE

To fly through the air for the greatest possible distance while wearing snow skis, and to do so with grace, style and stability, then land with something approaching the same qualities.

REWARDS

There's big money and adulation for top ski jumpers in northern and central Europe and some parts of North America (and, during the brief and perplexing Eddie the Eaglemania of the late 1980s, it was true in England, too). Gold, silver and bronze medals are up for grabs: the sport has been included in the Winter Olympics from the outset.

RISKS

Leaving the prescribed course at high speed and hitting something unprescribed. Losing air pressure beneath your skis, which can cause the body to overtake the skis and land first. Unintended and violent splits upon returning to land. Unintended anything else upon returning to land.

WHY?

It's fast, spectacular and technically fascinating—the skiers are actually flying, with the prone body and the purpose-designed skis acting as a wing and generating lift.

WHY NOT?

You can be a long way from the ground when you realise the jump is not going as well as you hoped. It is very hard to pull out at that point. The aesthetic element is highly subjective—jumping further than your opponents doesn't guarantee victory. It's discriminatory, too: the Olympics doesn't allow women. The original reason cited was for 'health concerns' though the latest excuse is 'due to the low number of female competitors'. Curling anyone?

THE RUNDOWN

Norwegians have been jumping on skis almost since they've been skiing on skis. In about 1860, a Norwegian carpenter and ski-maker named Sondre Norheim leapt over a snow-covered rock and sailed a distance of 30 metres to establish an early benchmark. Norheim became well-known for this and other skiing feats.

There was even a movie or two made about his life—hard to believe, yes, but ski jumpers have always been revered in certain countries. The best of today's crop have fan clubs, clothing lines and book and television deals.

The first formal ski jumping competition was held in 1862, and the event which would be labelled retrospectively 'The first Winter Olympics', International Winter Sports Week in France in 1924, included the sport.

In broad terms, the sport involves a skier sliding down an enormous and frighteningly steep ramp. This has a thin covering of grooved ice and skis are heavily waxed to reduce friction further. The skier will slide down the ramp while crouched tightly to be as aerodynamically efficient as possible and thereby achieve the highest speed. About 5 to 8 metres before the take-off point comes what has been described as 'the most powerful fraction of a second in sport'. The jumper springs forward and upward as he (and almost never she, according to the IOC) quickly moves the skis into position to maximise flying ability.

According to Espen Bredesen, the Norwegian who won gold and silver medals for ski jumping in the 1994 Winter Olympics, the 'in-run' is the critical phase of the jump:

> The speed increases very fast. You are doing nearly 90 kilometres per hour in just a couple of seconds, and when you come to the take-off you are pressed all together. If your position is right it will be just like being kicked out of the jump, if your position is a little bit, let's say 'blocked', you'll have no power through your legs and you'll make a bad jump.
>
> About 80 per cent of the length of the jump is practically all done at the take-off. After take-off you have to release your safety a little bit because your head is in front and the skis are beside you so you have no turning back. There is a couple of seconds after the take-off of each jump when you don't know whether you have the skis in front of you or under you and you are a little bit unsure how it is going to be.

Bredesen started early, building small ramps as a child and jumping 15 metres when he was ten years old. So what are the qualities that make a good ski jumper? 'They have better balance than other skiers maybe,' he says, 'but they don't have as much fear and can be with a little bit more adrenalin in their body. They always want to go to bigger hills, and jump further and higher.'

Over the years, different jumping techniques have come and gone. Early jumpers 'windmilled', which is to say spun their arms like pathetic flesh propellers, though this was for stability rather than for lift or forward motion. Then came the vogue for bending, which eventually saw competitors leaning over parallel skis in a jack-knife position with their arms by their sides and their noses hanging over the end of the skis. Since the 1990s, however, the top jumpers have held their skis in a V-position as if to say 'Up yours, gravity'.

Initially, this position was thought to be ungraceful and very poor aerodynamically. But skiers using it were achieving big distances and wind-tunnel testing soon showed that by spreading the skis and leaning at the right angle, the body could become part of the 'wing'. The flying V increased lift by 28 per cent over the parallel ski technique.

Miran Tepeš, now an official with the international ski body FIS, won an Olympic silver medal with parallel skis but admits the V is safer and more effective:

When you have skis apart you are less sensitive to the wind and other conditions. Before, if you got a wind gust, it hit first the skis, and the skis pushed your legs up and this turned you over. With the newer technique, when the gust comes it hits at the same time the body and the skis and it lifts you up. There are two surfaces that are influenced at the same time if there is turbulence in the air.

There is a couple of seconds after the take-off of each jump when you don't know whether you have the skis in front of you or under you and you are a little bit unsure how it is going to be.

Also making ski jumping less of a lottery is improved track design. Engineers now better match the fall of the landing area with the likely trajectory of the skiers, enabling skiers to travel further but lower. They now hover about three to four metres above the snow. Previously, to achieve winning distances, they had to sail through the air twice as high.

The participants themselves tend to be built a bit like gliders. Typically they are 1.8 metres tall but just 60 kilograms. As Tepeš puts it, 'no heavy birds can fly.'

Once in the air, ski jumpers steer by moving their arms. If they are well positioned at take-off, however, they don't need to do too much of it. The flight only lasts three to five seconds, at which point they hit the ground with a shock equal to three times their body weight.

Individual and team events are held at the Winter Olympics on the 'normal hill' and 'large hill'. The first has a 'K-point' (a badly spelled 'calculation' or 'critical' point) of between 75 and 99 metres. The K-point is a line in sand, so to speak, except that it's in the snow. In a K90 competition, if you cover less than 90 metres points are deducted. Exceed the 'par' and points are added. The large hill has a K-point of 120 metres.

Ski jumpers are judged not only on distance but style. They receive points for such things as keeping their skis steady during flight, holding a good body position and landing elegantly in the so-called Telemark manner (with one foot just ahead of the other to avoid falling forward, and knees bent to absorb impact).

Tepeš has had a few big crashes, breaking his back on one occasion, and smashing his face against the ground on another and shattering his cheek-bones:

Accidents happen sometimes because of the wind, sometimes because the athletes are willing to risk maybe too much. The further forward you lean from the take-off, the lower the air resistance, and you take more speed into the second phase of the flight. This is good, but if you stay too low the skis then don't come up enough and then you are in trouble.

At some point ski jumping becomes ski flying. Ski flying events take place on ramps with a K-point of 185 metres and greater. The biggest of the big is at Planica, Slovenia, where a jump of 239 metres has been recorded.

On a K120 hill the skiers take off at about 92–95 kilometres per hour. Depending on the wind direction, ski flyers can take off at 105 kilometres per hour and land at up to 125 kilometres per hour. Fast isn't necessarily good, though—an oncoming wind slows the skier down but provides more lift.

Espen Bredesen twice set ski flying records with 209 metres (1994) and 210 metres (1997). Back then, flyers used to sail as high as 12 metres off the deck. 'The first time I was scared. Who wouldn't be? Every coach says you are just to do the same thing as in a normal ski jump, but the mental balance is the difficult part.'

Once he had mastered it, Bredesen said every ski flying was 'just an incredible kick'. The 8 seconds seemed like much longer. 'You really enjoy the feeling and its like a payment for all the training … when you are jumping good it feels like you are floating, like you are being pressed up.'

It's also eerily quiet, he says. 'You can't hear spectators, can't hear anything. Maybe the wind, just a bit.'

A newer ski jumping variation is freestyle aerial skiing, a mix of acrobatics and ski jumping. The competitors (which can include women, even in the Olympics) fire off a short, sharp ramp and perform backward or forward somersaults with any combination of spins, twirls and twists. Distances are shorter but heights are just as great (the freestyle aerialists reach 4 metres). The chances of coming down headfirst are also increased.

Accidents happen sometimes because of the wind, sometimes because the athletes are willing to risk maybe too much.

POSSIBLE INJURIES

Modern tracks are much safer than older ones, and fortunately the obstacles people once hit during crashes—such as fences, photographers and spectators—have largely been removed from critical areas. However, the increased speeds and distances mean that when accidents happen they are big. With any 'off', broken bones are a strong possibility, along with concussion, compression injuries and even puncturing of the body by wayward skis. The biggest risk remains losing pressure beneath the skis once in the air. At a wind-marred World Cup meeting in Poland in early 2007 this happened to Czech Jan Mazoch. His skis were pushed behind him and he slammed into the ground head-first then slid unconscious to the bottom of the hill. Although Mazoch sustained severe swelling of the brain, he thankfully avoided permanent brain damage. Computer modelling from the Space Science and Engineering Center at the University of Wisconsin-Madison shows freestylers hit the ground harder than the traditional ski jumpers, even though the traditionalists are travelling further and at twice the speed. The 'landing shock' for a freestyle aerialist can be the equivalent of a 6.1-metre vertical fall onto a flat surface. That's the height of a two-storey building.

When Vinko Bogataj represented Yugoslavia in the 1970 International Ski Flying Championships, he decided to abort his run halfway down the ramp because he considered conditions unsafe. Bogataj tried to wipe off speed, instead speed wiped off Bogataj. He lost his balance then flipped, tumbled, spun, cartwheeled and generally looked like an exploding bucket of arms, legs and skis as he barrelled off the end of the ramp and through a retaining fence, almost taking out a clump of rather surprised spectators. The wayward Yugoslav was concussed but, miraculously, had no broken bones. Unbeknown to Bogataj, however, the big bad moment was captured by a film crew from America's 'Wide World of Sports' and the footage was spliced into the show's opening credits to match the narration '... and the agony of defeat'. There it stayed for two decades, making Bogataj's personal pile-up so famous he received an out-of-the-blue invitation to be the guest of honour at the television show's 30th anniversary dinner. On arrival Bogataj was positively stunned to find Muhammad Ali and others asking for his autograph.

Great heights: Thomas Morgenstern at Oberstdorf, Germany, in 2006.

Photo: rutgerpauw.com/Red Bull Photofiles

* Jan Boklov. *This Swedish skier was frantically searching for a way to gain a performance edge over Finland's Matti Nykänen, widely considered unbeatable. In 1985 Boklov came up with the flying V-position. Competitors and spectators laughed at first but Boklov soon showed that his method improved stability and lift. Boklov flew so far officials had to lower the starting point on some ramps. However, he didn't win to start with because judges considered the technique inelegant and marked him down for style. The flying V is now universal in top competition.*

* Matti Nykänen. *He won four Olympic Golds and more World Championships than any other skier during the 1980s. He is thought by many to be the greatest ski jumper ever. Unfortunately, he is thought by an equal number of people to be Finland's George Best. Nykänen followed his sports career by working as a singer, a sex-line worker and even a private stripper. His several marriages, jail terms for assault, insolvencies and wild alcoholic incidents are reflected in the title of the authorised biography* **On Top and in a Hole**. *Nykänen says in the foreword: 'This book must and should be read. It belongs on every bookshelf, right next to the Bible.' Thanks to his exploits and wonderful sense of proportion, Nykänen is by some estimates the single most written-about person in Finnish tabloids. A film,* **Matti**, *has been made about his life.*

* Bjørn Einar Romøren. *The king of ski flying, in 2005 Romøren recorded a world record jump of 239 metres, achieved at Planica in Slovenia. That's almost two-and-a-half football fields. Romøren, born in Norway in 1981, is also a multiple World Cup medal winner in more conventional ski jumping. A Finnish ski jumper and drag racer, Janne Ahonen, has covered 240 metres in his best jump but landed in what could best be described as a heap. The distance did not count as a result.*

* Eddie 'The Eagle' Edwards. *Twelve years before Eric 'The Eel' Moussambani's sporting ineptitude in the pool at the 2000 Sydney Olympics won people's hearts, there was Eddie the Eagle. The 24-year-old plasterer was the first Brit to compete in ski jumping at Olympic level. Overweight, underskilled and with such bad eyesight he had to wear thick glasses which immediately fogged up with the cold, Edwards flapped his arms in the air, and finished stone motherless last in his two events. After covering 71 metres in the K90 (the gold medal distance was 118.5 metres) he was dubbed a 'ski dropper' rather than a 'ski jumper'. Nonetheless, Reuters reported his 'cheerful embrace of mediocrity has captured the imagination of millions', and Edwards became a cult figure around the world. He attracted groupies and had hit records in Finland and England, despite not speaking Finnish—and struggling quite a bit with English. The Winter Olympic qualification conditions were later raised in what was known as the 'Eddie the Eagle Rule'.*

Gregor Schlierenzauer checks out his audience in Innsbruck, Austria, 2007.

Photo: GEPA Pictures/Red Bull Photofiles

Touching the sky:
Greg Mortimer atop
Manaslu, the eighth
highest mountain in
the world.

Photo: Greg Mortimer/
Aurora Expeditions

7

MOUNTAIN CLIMBING

100
MOUNTAIN CLIMBING

OBJECTIVE

To ascend a bloody big hill, have your photo taken at the pointy bit then make it down alive.

REWARDS

Primarily, bragging rights and personal satisfaction. A few climbers have become household names, though with more than 2000 people now having conquered the world's tallest mountain, Everest, it is hard to be noticed except through disaster (*Touching the Void* and *Into Thin Air* both became bestselling books then films based on catastrophes at high altitude). Most people who earn money from climbing either sell mountaineering equipment or guide richer but less accomplished people to the top of iconic mountains.

RISKS

The possibility of falling down cliffs, ravines, canyons, chasms, gullies, crevices, gorges, cols, glaciers, rocky slopes and anything else that hurts. Exposure to excessive, and perhaps fatal, cold. Making stupid and even terminal decisions due to the brain-numbing effects of oxygen deprivation. Being literally blown away by gales or even 200-knot jet-stream winds. There are also landslides, mudslides, rock-falls, avalanches and uncaring colleagues. In May 2006, 40 climbers walked past 34-year-old Briton David Sharp as he lay dying near the summit of Mount Everest.

WHY?

More than most activities, mountaineering is a personal challenge. It's about proving something to yourself and a small number of co-climbers, rather than to a crowd of spectators. It demands supreme concentration in the most extreme conditions known to man. It often requires life-and-death teamwork among people who are, by temperament, diehard loners. Climbers say the bonds formed are lifelong. There are no time limits (beyond those imposed by the weather and seasons), so a good climb can last weeks or even months. The scenery's tiptop, too. 'This is a thrilling business altogether,' the ever-so-English George Mallory wrote to his wife Ruth from the side of Everest in 1921. 'I can't tell you how it possesses me, and what a prospect it is. And the beauty of it all!'

WHY NOT?

When things go right you are out of sight, and when they go wrong you are a long way from help. It's hard and lonely work, dangerous, poorly paid and sometimes selfish (expensive and dangerous rescue operations are launched regularly to rescue climbers who either haven't done their homework properly, or have exceeded their abilities). Fatalities are increasing as more people pay to be escorted up Everest and the other big peaks despite lacking the necessary experience, a trend Tim Macartney-Snape has described as 'the antithesis of mountaineering'.

Scaling peaks can be expensive and bureaucratic, too; poor nations have high mountains and know how to charge for the right to climb them. Many beautiful places are now littered with oxygen tanks and other discarded climbing equipment, while rocks untouched for millions of years are punctured with bolts, or adorned with fixed lines and even permanent ladders.

THE RUNDOWN

In times gone by it was common knowledge that gods or monsters lived in tall mountains and that encroaching on their territory would bring down the wrath of either or both. That's not to say no-one ever climbed mountains, but most people did not consider it a sport, a leisure activity, or even something worth doing much before the eighteenth century.

It was then that European scientists started ascending the alps to study nature, the weather and the stars, and in 1760 a cash prize was offered for the first person to make it to the summit of Mont Blanc, the peak named after Europe's most expensive fountain pen. The prize was finally claimed in 1786.

By the 1850s 'Alpinism' was a popular activity, at least among wealthy people with lots of spare time. The tallest peaks in Europe were 'summited' one after another, then Europeans headed to the Americas and Africa in search of bigger highs. By the twentieth century it was acknowledged that the supreme challenges were in the Himalayas and British climbers in particular had set their sights on the big daddy of them all: the 8848-metre Mount Everest.

The first eight Everest expeditions were all from Old Blighty, beginning with an exploratory trip in 1921. In 1953 the bastard was finally knocked off, to use Edmund Hillary's famous phrase, albeit by Kiwi and Tibetan-born Nepali members of Colonel John Hunt's British expedition. An Italian team made it to the very top of the second-tallest mountain, K2, a year later. This received much less attention, but K2 (in Pakistan) is only 237 metres shorter than Everest and steeper and colder because of its more northerly position, and generally blighted with worse weather. It is thought by many to be the toughest mountain on Earth, and it would be another 23 years before any one else reached the top.

Once all the major peaks had been reached, climbers had to find new challenges. This they did by following more dangerous routes to the top, by working in smaller teams (or even solo), by forgoing existing technology such as supplementary oxygen tanks, or adopting new technology or techniques to scale sheer faces or terrifying overhangs earlier considered unpassable.

Everest remains a bastard to knock off, despite fixed lines, a ladder up the most difficult section (popularly named The Hillary Step), and all manner of lightweight and efficient modern materials and equipment. With that in mind, it is hard to believe the British expedition of 1924 came so close in tweed jackets and lace-up leather boots. Even the successful 1953 team had equipment that was almost laughable by today's standards, and they had to carry heavy canvas tents and hemp ropes. They were also going into the unknown, which makes everything harder.

At high altitude the simplest tasks are difficult. Your body doesn't work the same way. On Everest we were all extremely fit and five steps was the limit of our ability.

Australian climber Tim Macartney-Snape has written that above 8000 metres even the best climbers 'begin to feel twinges of losing control. Your pattern of thoughts are more dreamlike, difficult to direct, the brain's ability to think is slowed and complex thoughts are difficult to grasp.'

Greg Mortimer was Macartney-Snape's climbing partner on the first Australian summiting of Everest. He agrees:

At high altitude the simplest tasks are difficult. Your body doesn't work the same way. On Everest we were all extremely fit and five steps was the limit of our ability. Your body suffers oxygen debt and you have to stop for a couple minutes to get back enough oxygen, and the first part of that is gasping desperately. Your lips go blue, your speech can be slurred, your thought patterns can be slow. I know that from seeing video of myself, and not realising it at the time. It is a gradual process. Vision blurs for some people ... you don't want to eat, you have to force yourself, and anything with any strong taste is repulsive.

'It all sounds pretty bloody awful,' he adds with a quiet laugh. 'The upside is way and above all those things ... it is more than worth it.'

Mortimer, who has also climbed K2 and Annapurna II, says it is a source of great humility to come face to face with the 'raw edge of big mountains':

Climbing mountains is essentially how I interpret the world: the personal testing, the problem solving, the interaction with nature, the interaction with other people, man's place in the world, our frailty in the world in the big picture and the way we interpret our sense of ego. Climbing mountains is a great way to learn about these things.

Aside from that, after climbing a big mountain with no oxygen, your body is juiced up with lots and lots of oxygen molecules for about six weeks and you are at a heightened sense of awareness, you've got a great sense of achievement and the luxury of everyday life is, well, verdant.

To some it may sound a little like hitting yourself on the head because it feels good when you stop. And how does anyone enjoy themselves on those mountains where statistics show the chances of being killed are frighteningly high?

According to Mortimer, 'Mountaineers think it's not going to happen to them. Death is not ever-present. It doesn't feel like that. It's much more exuberant than that. The feeling is much more of excitement and calm watchfulness, rather than sword of Damocles hanging over your head.'

Mountaineering attracts a more cerebral crowd than many sports. There is a strong body of literature written by mountaineers, perhaps because it is an activity that affords a lot of time for contemplation by often introspective characters.

Although the most iconic challenge has always been Everest, *Touching the Void* (Joe Simpson's account of disaster in the Peruvian Andes) and many other books, films and documentaries show that it is possible to expose yourself to just as much mountaineering difficulty and danger in scores of other places.

Some people talk about 'assaulting' a peak but often find it is the peak itself that mounts an assault, usually occasioning bodily harm. Mortimer says: 'Mountains are a really graphic example of where showing off or a sense of bravado doesn't work, spectacularly—people die all the time with that mindset.'

In higher altitudes, mountaineers are almost never entirely dry, warm or well. In BASE jumping the risk lasts only a few seconds, but on a mountainside it is possible to be in mortal danger for days or even weeks. And unlike, say, motorcycle racing, when someone has 'an off', the yellow flags don't come out so the stretcher, painkillers and neck-braces can be rushed to the spot. Often severely injured people need to keep going—and coming down is every bit as dangerous as going up.

Some have described summits as anticlimactic, but I have been lucky never to have experienced anything but unbounded joy on them.

POSSIBLE INJURIES

Broken bones, severe bruising, wind burn, snow blindness. Loss of fingers, toes, noses and lips through frostbite. Death through hypothermia or sudden impact. Hypoxia caused by the oxygen shortage at high altitudes can lead to seizures, coma and death, or long-term brain damage. Other medical risks include high-altitude pulmonary oedema (swelling and/or fluid build-up in the lungs) and high-altitude cerebral oedema (swelling of the brain tissue due to fluid leakage), both of which can be fatal.

In the Himalayas the Sherpa guides have the highest death rate as they often push themselves harder, sometimes have inferior equipment and are less likely to turn back for fear of losing much-needed wages or future employment. More than 180 people have died climbing Everest and there are still as many as 120 corpses up there. In 2006 Swede Tomas Olsson died on an expedition to ski down the treacherous North Face.

Opposite: The idea of a pleasant afternoon's recreation is not the same for mountain climbers as it is for people who prefer the flat bits in between. This is Greg Mortimer having fun at Stoney Middleton in the Peak District in England.

Photo: Greg Mortimer/Aurora Expeditions

The first man to 'knock off' a mountain of more than 8000 metres was Frenchman Maurice Herzog. He climbed Annapurna in Nepal in 1950 without oxygen, and without knowing exactly where he was. The first few weeks of the expedition involved searching out a route into the Himalayas and the mountain Herzog eventually climbed was not the one he was aiming for. The team doctor was giving Herzog small and slightly mysterious pills to keep him going. These may account for the dreamy tone Herzog adopted when later describing his amazing feat, and the fact he somehow managed to lose his gloves near the summit yet didn't feel cold. When Herzog returned to camp and shook hands with those keen to congratulate him, they interrupted his incessant, cheery talking to mention his fingers were 'violet and white and hard as wood'. It didn't worry Herzog, by his account he was 'blissfully floating on a sea of joy remote from reality'. Many rank his climb as more difficult and daring than the Everest conquest three years later. It cost Herzog most of his toes and fingers.

TRULY MAD MOMENTS

* Edmund Hillary and Tenzing Norgay.

On 29 May 1953, this pair became New Zealand's most famous beekeeper and Nepal's most famous Sherpa. It wasn't the original script that Hillary and 'Sherpa Tenzing' would be the first to reach the top of Mount Everest but they proved stronger, fitter and more capable than the other members of the expedition. Less well-known is that Hillary—even his name sounds steep—'summited' many other difficult peaks, made it to both Poles and blasted a jet boat along the Ganges from the Himalayas to the ocean.

* Reinhold Messner.

The famed Italian adventurer is considered by many the greatest mountaineer of all time. Messner was the first man to climb all 14 of the world's 8000-metre-plus mountains. He pioneered the ascent of Everest without supplementary oxygen (with Peter Habeler in 1978) and in 1980 was the first to climb it solo without supplementary oxygen. His career was always haunted by accusations he left his brother to die on a mountain in Pakistan in 1970, though the finding of Günther Messner's remains in 2005 seemed to support Reinhold's version of events. Messner has written 40 books, one of them detailing his claimed encounters with the yeti.

* Aleister Crowley.

The infamous English occultist, writer, bisexual and drug-hoover of the early twentieth century, popularly known as the 'most wicked man alive', was also a fanatical mountaineer. He attempted K2, the world's second-highest mountain, as early as 1902, though he didn't reach the summit. In 1905 he was part of the first ever attempt on the world's third-highest mountain, Nepal's Khangchenjunga. Although Crowley again failed to reach the top, he ascended as high as 6500 metres.

* Tim Macartney-Snape.

In 1984 Macartney-Snape and Greg Mortimer became the first Australians to reach the summit of Mount Everest, and they did it without oxygen, without Sherpa assistance and via a new route. Even more remarkably, in 1990 Macartney-Snape became the first man to walk from sea level to the top of Everest. In his account of that experience, **Everest: From Sea to Summit**, he wrote: 'Some mountaineers have described summits as anticlimactic, but I feel I have been lucky never to have experienced anything but unbounded joy on them. Never has the miracle and beauty of life been so real and vivid as on a mountaintop in clear weather'.

* George Mallory and Andrew Irvine.

This pair was last seen alive heading for the Everest summit as part of the 1924 British expedition, but it was never established whether or not they made it. (Edmund Hillary later conceded that it was possible they did, but added that getting down alive was also an important part of a 'complete first ascent'.) In 1999 Mallory's frozen body was found at 8170 metres or 678 metres below the summit. Alas, there was no sign of his camera, which may have proved that either he or Irvine reached the top (on balance, though, most experts believe neither did). It was Mallory's third visit to Everest; he at first thought using supplementary oxygen was unsporting, perhaps even un-British. He was eventually persuaded it was the only way to get to the top.

An amazingly exposed
tent city on K2 in
Pakistan.

Photo: Greg Mortimer/
Aurora Expeditions

'What seems a wild scrimmage is in fact full of manoeuvres' said buzkashi witness Dr Jacob Bronowski. To new observers, though, still seems like a wild scrimmage.

Photo: Dr Whitney Azoy

8

BUZKASHI

OBJECTIVE

To scoop up by hand the carcass of a beheaded, disembowelled and de-hoofed goat or calf from horseback and maintain control of said carcass long enough to ride 'clear and free'. This is to be done while being pursued by other riders who are armed with whips and not afraid to use them.

REWARDS

Fame, prestige and prize money, though only in Afghanistan and a few surrounding areas. In traditional times, a good rider, or chapandaz, was employed by a local warlord and presumably well paid, or at least allowed to live. The real stars though are the horses and horse-owners. An Afghani maxim, 'better a poor rider on a good horse than a good rider on a poor horse', removes the need for a salary cap.

RISKS

Being thrown off your horse and trampled, or being hit, kicked, whipped or worse by other competitors. Finding that the game you are in has escalated into a larger conflict taking in tribal, ethnic or religious rivalries. At that point, serious weaponry is likely to appear.

WHY?

Buzkashi is fast and furious. It involves tactical skills and great horsemanship—both considered hugely important among Afghans. It's democratic, too: some games involve as many players as turn up, and that may be many hundreds. Ageism clearly has no place as some of the best players are 40 and above. Buzkashi is also living history, a sport that has survived for hundreds of years unaffected by technology.

WHY NOT?

The words 'graceful' and 'buzkashi' are rarely used together. It is not exactly family entertainment, and not only because women are not allowed to watch (though frequently do). Newer players rarely make it even close to the carcass. The lack of a marked-out field in many competitions means the players can stray from spectator's view; even if they stay close, the carcass can be obscured by the dust and sheer number of horsemen. The sport is highly political, too, with various governments either banning or sponsoring the sport at various times for political gain. Khans, warlords and mujahedin commanders, too, have staged buzkashi contests as demonstrations of might and influence. In short, everything about buzkashi concerns fierce rivalry at every level, and real-life violence is never far away. That is why it has often been used as a metaphor for Afghani politics.

THE RUNDOWN

They are a tough lot, the Afghans. As the conveniently out-of-copyright Joseph Rudyard Kipling was once moved to observe: 'When you're wounded and left on Afghanistan's plains/and the women come out to cut up what remains/jest roll to your rifle and blow out your brains/and go to your Gawd like a soldier.'

Unsurprisingly, the Afghani national sport reflects the country's tough history. Buzkashi, which is translated as 'goat dragging' or 'goat grabbing', probably has its origins in the practice of swooping down from horseback to steal lambs, goats and calves. The nomadic Turkic people brought the practice—and the game—to Afghanistan as they spread west from Mongolia and China.

Buzkashi involves matching an expert rider or chapandaz with a highly trained horse. These horses know to stop and wait when the rider falls off, and will accelerate fiercely if and when the rider picks up the carcass. Often a calf is used instead of a buz or 'goat', as it is tougher.

In the early 1970s, during the filming of the landmark television series 'The Ascent of Man', writer/narrator Dr Jacob Bronowski attended a game of buzkashi, which his team filmed beautifully in colour. Bronowski explained that the players don't form teams:

> The object is not to prove one group better than the other but to find a champion. No quarter is given, this is not a sporting event, there is nothing in the rules about fair play. The tactics are pure Mongol, a discipline of shock.

One reason fair play isn't in the rules is because there are very few rules. Riders are frequently knocked off their horses, and the whips and sticks intended to motivate the horses are often pressed into service against other competitors.

That said, whipping the face or body is generally frowned upon, though whipping hands and forearms is routine.

There have been reports—without a lot of historical back-up, it should be said—that the game has been played with live prisoners and/or the corpses of tribal enemies. Such probable exaggerations aside, the game is still hugely fierce and tough. Adding to the general degree of difficulty is the dust thrown up by galloping, wheeling horses and the fact that the carcass is often weighted with sand and can weigh up to 60 kilograms.

Former American diplomat Dr Whitney Azoy studied the sport as an anthropologist for two years in the 1970s (most first-person reports by westerners are from that time because the country has been at war continually since then). Azoy then wrote what is still the standard English language reference: *Buzkashi: Game and Power in Afghanistan*. Describing a typical game, he wrote:

> *Lunging half-blind in the melée, one rider manages to grab hold of the carcass briefly but, as a saying goes, 'Every calf has four legs' and other riders quickly wrench it away. The calf is trampled, dragged, tugged, lifted and lost again as one competitor after another seeks to gain sole control.*

Now the centre director and senior fellow at the American Institute of Afghanistan Studies, Dr Azoy, is based in Kabul about six months per year, and still believes buzkashi is the wildest game in the world, 'a Hobbesian war of all against all':

No quarter is given, there is nothing in the rules about fair play. The tactics are pure Mongol, a discipline of shock.

I can't think of a game which is played with more muscle power—and I'm talking about the horses as well as the men—a game which is as rough and tumble, a game with the same potential for real-life violence. Because you've got everybody already pushing and shoving and yelling and screaming and battering the hell out of each other in the name of fun. If there's a dispute that involves real-world rivalries, then all this pushing and screaming and battering and so forth very quickly becomes no longer for fun, it becomes for real.

The politics of how fights are settled, and by whom, is a major aspect of the game, Dr Azoy says:

Most disputes are settled relatively amicably ... occasionally a dispute is not settled. Then typically what happens, sometimes after outright fighting with knives and occasionally with guns, is one of the factions at the game will ride away in disgust, maybe in cowardice, but ostensively in disgust, saying that the people who sponsored the buskashi didn't know how to do it. They may be leaving because they are vastly outnumbered and scared, but they'll never admit to that.

Although there are no teams in traditional buzkashi, ad hoc alliances form and dissolve repeatedly as the game plays out. The way to win is to gain sole control of the carcass and ride 'clear and free'. Unfortunately, that's a term vague enough to ensure not everyone thinks the game has finished at the same time as the man who thinks he has just won. Yet, as Dr Bronowski observed, 'The astonishing thing of the game is what routed the armies that faced the Mongols: that what seems a wild scrimmage is in fact full of manoeuvres and dissolves suddenly with the winner riding clear.'

Dr Azoy's two-year absorption in buzkashi saw him become one of the few foreigners to participate in the sport:

People were very good to me, they accepted me pretty well and protected me not only off the field but also on. Usually I'd be on horseback around the outside, but every once in a while—I don't know why, it was utter folly—I simply tried to ride my way in the middle. Twice, to my dismay, I found myself more or less in the way of the carcass. I grabbed hold of it and on both occasions a friend [an Afghan rider] was right there and he grabbed hold of me and said 'Whitney, let this damn thing go'.

Dr Azoy admits he has no idea what would have been the consequence of holding on to it. 'They may have cut me some slack but there was money on the table and these guys aren't rich ...'

The atmosphere out on a buzkashi field is tumultuous, he says:

Most of the noise is the noise of the horses, but you'll hear people shouting and they'll encourage their horses with an incongruously soft hiss, when trying to persuade their horses to get right to the middle. And they'll be yelling encouragement to themselves and those people with whom they vaguely feel affinity.

Dr Azoy says the most common serious injuries are broken bones in legs, shoulders and ankles:

Occasionally a person will get crushed. I knew a man whose father was a prominent rider who died when he leaned over the saddle horn and a horse landed on top of his back and in effect the saddle horn punctured the man's sternum and he died soon after. But you don't have many deaths in the game, and of the deaths you have, at least as many of them come from fighting as from playing.

You don't have many deaths in the game, and of the deaths you have, at least as many of them come from fighting as from playing.

From the 1950s a government-sponsored form of buzkashi evolved. This divided the players into two teams (usually of no more than a dozen a side) and established formal boundaries, uniforms, referees and circles marked out as 'goals'. Players had to grab the carcass, carry it around a marker flag, then drop it in the 'goal', otherwise known as the 'circle of justice'. Tactics such as deliberately whipping other players or knocking them off their horses were strictly forbidden. For purists, this is the one-day cricket of buzkashi, and it caught on only in the major cities.

Dr Azoy says that although this new form still exists, the government is so weak it doesn't really sponsor games. Furthermore, he says, 'buzkashi never becomes a team sport, barely even in the government form of the game, which is built on teams.'

In rural areas and the north, buzkashi is still the traditional 'anything goes' version.

POSSIBLE INJURIES

Whip welts, impact injuries, broken bones and, occasionally, death. The horses get a hard time, too. And let's not think about the goat. Some buzkashi games were strafed by Soviet airpower during the 1980s and, even today, those who venture too far off the track face the real risk of unexploded ordnance. The Russians alone planted more than ten million anti-personnel mines in Afghanistan during their ten-year occupation.

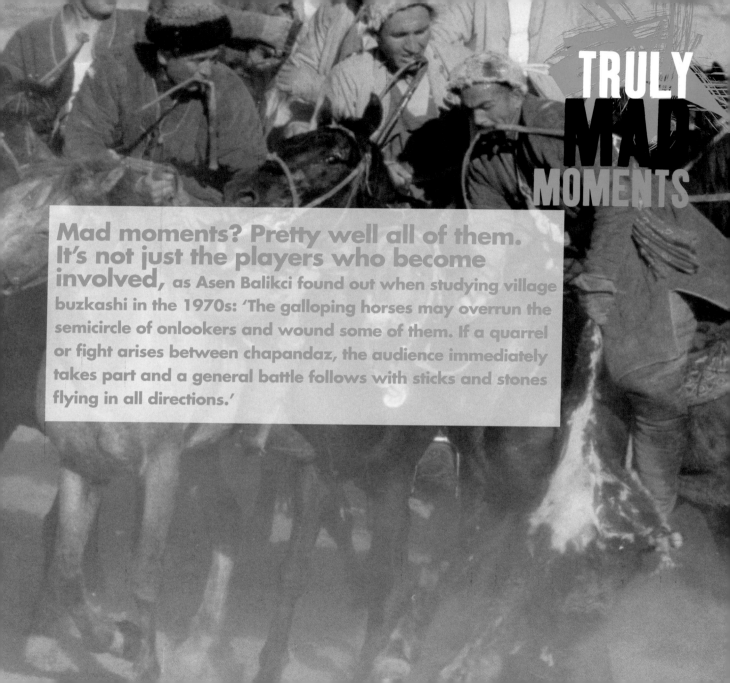

Mad moments? Pretty well all of them. It's not just the players who become involved, as Asen Balikci found out when studying village buzkashi in the 1970s: 'The galloping horses may overrun the semicircle of onlookers and wound some of them. If a quarrel or fight arises between chapandaz, the audience immediately takes part and a general battle follows with sticks and stones flying in all directions.'

* **Genghis Khan.** *Arguably the spiritual father of the game. According to the Federation of Sports of Afghanistan, buzkashi is possibly a re-enactment of the campaigns of 'the great Mongol and his Golden Horde in Asia Minor'. Khan's Mongol horsemen were notorious for arriving at enemy campsites at full gallop and swooping down to grab livestock and other loot and plunder. 'One theory,' says the Federation's sporting handbook, 'is that in retaliation, the inhabitants of northern Afghanistan established a mounted defence against the raids and this practice might be the direct forbearer of today's Buzkashi.'*

* **Jabar.** *A highly talented horseman or chapandaz mentioned by academic and film-maker Asen Balikci in the 1970s. Jabar was offered large sums by Awkhana Pashtuns to switch from local ethnic rivals the Kogaday Hazara. However, in a typical quirk of the buzkashi 'transfer system' Jabar had to be guaranteed protection against violent reprisals from his former employers. Despite bidding and flattery wars over a good chapandaz, it is the horses and the horse-owners who take most of the glory. Much pride is involved; it was explained to Balikci that 'it is better to shoot a horseowner with a gun straight in the face than telling him loudly on the buzkashi arena that his horse is weak and did not run fast enough.'*

* **Jack Palance and Omar Sharif.** *OK, it was only a movie—John Frankenheimer's* **The Horsemen** *(1971)—and it failed dismally at the US box office, probably because it was set in Kabul, Afghanistan, and there were no American characters in the story. Palance and Sharif played father and son respectively, the latter attempting to secure the former's respect by equalling his feats in the buzkashi arena. A clichéd scenario, sure, but the many 'goat dragging' scenes are superb. The review by famed film critic Roger Ebert remarked, 'there hasn't been a sustained action sequence on this scale since the chariot race in* **Ben Hur***, which you may be reminded of.'*

The wildest game in the world? Up to 800 riders have been known to join a single game of buzkashi. The goat is somewhere bottom centre.

Photo: Dr Whitney Azoy

A participant in the
Red Bull Speed Run
in Austria in 2001
hits 130 kilometres
per hour just a couple
of metres from the
ground. The event
was won by Austrian
hang gliding champion
Manfred Ruhmer, who
has flown over 700
kilometres in a single
hop.

Photo: Bernhard Spöttel/Red
Bull Photofiles

9

HANG GLID ING

OBJECTIVE
To fly from the ground using nothing but the wind for power and soar like an eagle.

REWARDS

The pure joy of silent, fuel-free, unassisted human flight. 'To fly with a pair or wings, it's a dream come true,' says Australian hang-gliding pioneer Bill Moyes. 'It's better than anything else you can do.'

RISKS

Soaring not like an eagle but a brick. Hitting trees, power lines or even other hang gliders. Flying well but landing badly: feet pointing upwards like a dead fly is a particularly bad look.

WHY?

It has made reality the dreams of the early birdmen, those brave, foolhardy souls who strapped on wings and launched themselves into the air (almost inevitably as a brief prelude to launching themselves into the ground).

WHY NOT?

It's impractical (it can't be done just anywhere, nor do you always end up where you intended) and not something that lends itself to head-to-head competition.

THE RUNDOWN

NASA scientist Francis Rogallo developed a 'flexible winged kite' with the objective of bringing the early spacecraft back to Earth with a soft landing. It was eventually decided to use conventional parachutes, but Rogallo's design had a far broader influence than he could have imagined.

It was directly responsible for the hang-gliding craze of the 1960s and 1970s. His work inspired John Dickenson, an Australian, to build a personal hang glider. Dickenson spent $24 on his first model but kept developing the concept through the 1960s until it went from being an extremely dangerous novelty to a slightly less dangerous novelty.

In those early days hang gliding was considered a branch of water skiing, as most flights were launched behind speedboats. Bill Moyes was Dickenson's original test pilot. Short of defusing bombs in a sniper zone with a target pinned to your back, it is hard to think of a more dangerous job than being a hang-glider guinea pig in the 1960s. However, Moyes survived and says he loved every minute of it, even if he lost 'months, even years, to hospitalisation'.

As well as being unusually daring, Moyes was gifted. He set many early height and distance records and, in 1969, flew into the Grand Canyon, causing a sensation and helping bring hang gliding to a much larger audience in the United States.

By this time Moyes was touring American fairgrounds, demonstrating the new flying machines. Others followed in his wake and there were 17 fatalities among 'hang glider stuntmen' in a very short period of time. Moyes himself had five serious accidents in that period and such demonstrations were banned. By the mid-1970s, however, despite the fatalities, hang gliding was becoming something close to a mainstream sport, with foot launching now the most popular method of taking off.

Dickenson hadn't been the only one working on the idea and he and many other designers and engineers added innovations that improved safety and controllability, and increased strength while reducing weight.

Most designers and manufacturers adopted the superior 'gravity shift' system of steering (invented by Dickenson and improved by Moyes, who himself had become a leading hang-glider constructor), yet the number of accidents continued to climb. The biggest risk was stalling, a condition that occurred when the wing was tilted too far and lost its 'lift'. At that point the early hang gliders would immediately head for the ground by the most direct route. Says Moyes:

Everyone was building them and everyone was flying them. In 1975 there were so many fatalities—like one a week. Probably 1976 was the worst year. It was then the manufacturers' association was formed. Gliders had to pass stability tests.

More than 100 manufacturers couldn't meet the new standards and went out of business. The biggest advance was the compulsory incorporation of stall recovery systems. The sport suddenly became a lot safer and by the 1980s hang gliders had flown off Mount Kilimanjaro and the side of Everest and, elsewhere, had shown they could soar kilometres above their launching point. They seemed to be everywhere: up and down the coast, floating on sea breezes, and inland rising almost magically on thermal currents.

Top pilots can now do full barrel rolls and other obscenely show-offy manoeuvres. They can also exceed 130 kilometres per hour. They are helped by the fact that modern hang gliders are very strong. They are made of aircraft-grade aluminium and stainless steel with the sail (or wing) usually made from Dacron. Cables and wires make them even tougher, most have hand-deployed emergency 'chutes and some even have rocket-deployed 'chutes.

Another innovation that improved safety was the tandem hang glider. Originally students had to do everything on their own—now they can experience difficult manoeuvres first hand before trying them solo.

For Tony Armstrong, a former Australian Freestyle Champion (and now a hang-gliding instructor), it all started with the simple desire to fly. 'It's very peaceful up there, very independent. It's total freedom,' he says. Since taking his first flights in 1979, Armstrong has flown at a height of 6000 metres and has completed flights that lasted for six hours. He says freestyle competition 'is an expression of the whole flight dynamic':

> When you do manoeuvres you are losing altitude as you do them, so you've got to try to match your manoeuvres with the conditions you are working with. If you've got plenty of lift you can do big manoeuvres ... things like the full loop, that take a lot of energy, that need a lot of airspeed.

It's very peaceful up there, very independent. It's total freedom.

Sometimes things go wrong, and when they do you hit the ground and when you hit the ground, things break.

Armstrong has had 'some shitty landings—what we call "an arrival"', but has managed to avoid major injuries.

'I've had a couple of grazed knees, but before this I played professional rugby league. Back then I had knee reconstructions and broken arms and the full cahoot.'

Modern variations are blurring the gliding-flying-jumping lines. BASE jumpers and sky divers wearing wingsuits are achieving longer and longer 'flights'. Some wing-suiters are working towards landing hang-glider style, without a parachute.

In 2003 Austrian mechanic and extreme sportsman Felix Baumgartner was dropped from a plane, 9800 metres above the English port of Dover. With a V-shaped carbon fibre wing strapped to his back he pointed himself in the direction of France. Fourteen minutes later he was about 1000 metres above Calais, at which point he popped a 'chute and landed. He had reached a peak speed of 360 kilometres per hour during the 35-kilometre journey.

POSSIBLE INJURIES

Bill Moyes says of his exploits in the early days: 'Sometimes things go wrong, and when they do you hit the ground and when you hit the ground, things break. I've twice broken my pelvis and I've got two artificial knees now, and screws in one elbow and a broken shoulder and a few vertebrates damaged. But I still get around.' He stresses that the sport has become 'much much safer' since the barnstorming days: 'Insurance companies had us rated at 78 deaths per hundred thousand hours of activity, but now we are down to 3 or 4 deaths per hundred thousand hours.'

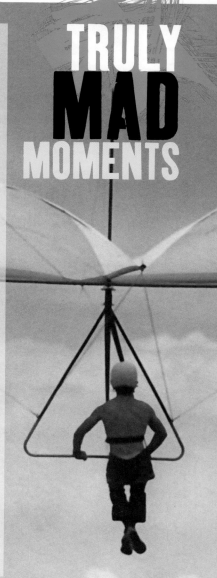

Known as the 'human condor', Italy's Angelo d'Arrigo used a series of hang gliders and ultra-light powered aircraft to travel with wild birds over immense distances. In 2004 he and his specially adapted hang glider were towed by an 'ultra light' to more than 9 kilometres above sea level, just 500 metres south of the Mount Everest summit. It was d'Arrigo's second attempt to overfly Everest and this time he was hit by severe turbulence and the tow link broke. Seconds later he disappeared into cloud. The temperature was -53 degrees, so cold that frozen tears were blocking much of his vision, but d'Arrigo made it over the summit and flew back a second time despite the turbulence. That wasn't necessarily the hardest bit. The rate of fall was so great in the thin air that d'Arrigo (further weighed down by oxygen tanks and other equipment) always knew he would have to land somewhere on the mountain, and probably at a speed of about 100 kilometres per hour. His hang glider was equipped with wheels and he brought it down safely on an ice field, though still at a freezing, gasping altitude of 6500 metres. Angelo D'Arrigo died in March 2006 while a passenger in a light aircraft.

Early days: a 1975 shot of pilot Miles Fagerlie near Flagstaff, Arizona. Note the 'swing seat' harness. Despite the remarkably relaxed posture, they were dangerous days.   Photo: Wikipedia Commons

* Otto Lilienthal. *A German who invented the hang glider in the early 1890s and became its first fatality in 1896. His gliders were the first true heavier-than-air flying machines. After as many as 2000 short and low flights, Lilienthal managed to attain a height of 17 metres—and then fall when a gust of wind snapped one of his wings. Before dying he reportedly said 'sacrifices have to be made'.*

* Lawrence Hargrave. *A genius of early aviation who managed to lift himself about 5 metres above the slopes of Stanwell Park, south of Sydney, in 1894. His 'manlift kite' was made up of four of his self-designed box kites linked by rope and fitted with a seat. Hargrave invented curved aerofoils and more, but as a gentleman inventor with a passion for the advancement of mankind, he communicated his ideas widely and never applied for a patent. The Wright Brothers and many others were beneficiaries of his work. Stanwell Park is now one of Australia's most popular hang-gliding sites.*

* Leo Valentin. *A French sky diving pioneer, credited by some as making sky diving a sport after World War Two by introducing techniques to make stable freefall possible. In some ways Valentin was the link between the early birdmen and the modern hang-glider pilots, testing gliders in a wind tunnel and achieving flight with a variety of different rigid and flexible wings. Unfortunately, while jumping out of a plane in 1956, Valentin struck the fuselage with one of his wings. He went into a spin and fell to his death.*

* Steve Moyes. *In 1982, with his father, Bill, Steve took his hang glider to the summit of Mount Kilimanjaro, the highest free-standing mountain in the world, and jumped off. The pair glided for 80 minutes, like a modern Daedalus and Icarus, though with better results as they both reached the ground safely. They had flown from an altitude of 5900 metres to the Tanzanian city of Moshi on the slopes below at just 1500 metres. Steve went on to be one of the world's most successful competition hang-glider pilots.*

* Larry Tudor. *An American multiple world-record holder who recorded an altitude gain of 4343 metres above California in 1985. Such a rise was almost unfathomable to the many who still considered the hang glider a mere novelty. In 1990 Tudor flew 488.2 kilometres from New Mexico to Kansas; four years later he beat his own distance record, flying 496 kilometres. The world record is now 700.6 kilometres; achieved by Austria's Manfred Ruhmer.*

Taking to the sky on a
wing. Prayer optional.

Photo: David Corby 2006/
Wikipedia Commons

Tow-in Tassie: Ross
Clarke-Jones taking on
the power of nature off
Tasmania in 2001.

Photo: Hilton Dawe/Red Bull
Photofiles

10

BIG WAVE SURFING

OBJECTIVE

To be towed onto the most enormous waves in the world, and stay on the dry side of them thanks to a small Kevlar–composite board strapped to your feet.

REWARDS

Big-dollar contracts and international travel for the top surfers, thanks largely to humungous sales of big wave DVDs. Other competitors still enjoy being at one with some of the mightiest forces of nature.

RISKS

Death by rinse cycle, being harpooned by your own board, being skewered on coral or thrown against an underwater rock the size of a bus by a pile of water the size of a building. There's also a real danger of sunburn and chapped lips.

WHY?

Few activities are more spectacular visually. Every wave varies in size, speed and angle of approach, so you can't keep trying the same wave until you have mastered it, as you would a corner on a motor racing circuit. This means the art of surfing is very much 'of the moment'. Add weather and other variables and it is hard to beat for immediacy and unpredictability.

WHY NOT?

You are totally dependent on the wind, waves and tides doing the right thing at the right moment. Surfing the biggest waves generally requires a support crew of smoky jet skis and noisy helicopters. Some believe this is debasing a simple man-and-nature sport.

THE RUNDOWN

The Polynesian islanders probably invented board surfing. Historians believe people were catching waves in Hawaii in 400AD—a time when most Europeans were up to their knees in mud and bunkering down for half a millennium of Dark Ages. Board surfing was first described to Europeans by Lieutenant James King of the Royal Navy in 1779. He noted that Hawaiian men who were 'almost amphibious' achieved 'a most astonishing velocity' on their planks and that the practice gave them great pleasure. 'On first seeing this very dangerous diversion,' King wrote in his diary, 'I did not conceive it possible but that some of them must be dashed to mummy against the sharp rocks.'

In the twentieth century, the legendary Hawaiian Olympic swimmer, Duke Kahanamoku, became the sport's ambassador. In 1914 he showed Australians how to board surf in a demonstration at Sydney's Freshwater Beach. However, it was the film *Gidget*, 45 years later, that kicked off the worldwide surfing boom.

As a well as a 'look' (in which, alas, Hawaiian shirts played a major part), surfing soon gained a soundtrack. This weird hybrid of slightly Middle Eastern-influenced melodies played on twangy guitars was soon embellished with barbershop quartet harmonies by The Beach Boys, a Californian band that had shaped its image around the sport, even though few members of the group were actually waterproof. Thomas Edison had filmed surfers at Waikiki Beach as early as 1898—starting the trend for surf movies, which as time went on would become longer, more boring and filled with ever more pretentious music. There are notable exceptions, however, including the fun of *Big Wednesday* and the doco-awesomeness of *Riding Giants*.

Early surfers did their stuff on large wooden planks. In the 1960s—by which time *Gidget* sequels included *Gidget Goes Hawaiian* and the less obvious *Gidget Goes to Rome*—surfers were using smaller, fibreglass boards. By the 1990s many surfers were clipping themselves onto short, manoeuvrable boards so they could perform freestyle tricks echoing those seen on skateboards and sailboards. But the most extreme branch of the sport, and the one requiring the most bravery, involved finding the mightiest waves on the planet and attempting to ride them. Early on this was done close to shore, and many sites—for example, Maverick's in California—offered not only magnificent waves but also an underwater cornucopia of jagged rocks, coral or caves ready to rip you to pieces or hold you down during a wipe-out.

A major revolution in big wave surfing came with the use of jet skis to tow riders into waves that previously couldn't be ridden simply because they were too big, too fast or too far from shore. Add to this advanced weather monitoring and suddenly you had mad keen surfers being helicoptered a hundred kilometres off the Spanish coast in mid-winter to catch waves that few would otherwise know existed.

The most famous tow-in sites are Hawaii's mega-scary Jaws, off the island of Maui, and Outside Log Cabins off Oahu. Several times a year the weather and underwater topography collude to produce near-perfectly formed waves of monstrous size. There is some argument about methods of measurement, but by most estimates these spots can produce 15- to 18-metre waves (that's the size of the swell), that give a 'face' of up to 26 metres from crest to trough. Once surfers have executed the final whip off the back of the jet ski, they experience either the ride of their life or the wipe-out that makes them believe they are about to end it.

In 1998, highly respected Australian big wave surfer Ross Clarke-Jones took on the so-called 'Biggest Wednesday' in Hawaii. He remembers that his first wave, at Outside Log Cabins, felt like 'a couple of football fields being titled at an angle … I had never seen a wave that big'. The speed achieved on the monster waves is about 80 kilometres per hour but, says Clarke-Jones, 'it feels like 200' and makes him feel 'more alive than anything … happier, more complete, more satisfied'. No matter how big the waves, Clarke-Jones says he doesn't feel any fear:

> Just excitement, a complete feeling of excitement. You are pretty much down to sight and touch, the other senses are all eliminated. You don't really hear it, you don't hear a thing. But your eyes are pretty wide open. I can't remember blinking.

You are pretty much down to sight and touch, the other senses are all eliminated. You don't really hear a thing. But your eyes are pretty wide open. I can't remember blinking.

Tow-in surfing is more about dislocating body parts really. The force of those waves can snap your back or rip your arms completely off their hinges.

And what does a wipe-out feel like? Ken Bradshaw provided one of the best descriptions to *Nature* magazine:

It feels like getting hit by a car, a soft car, and then spun around in a washing machine. This all happens in complete darkness, so that once you stop spinning you're presented with the challenge of finding your equilibrium and figuring out which way is up. Not to mention the pressure change: You can be pushed from the water's surface 50 feet down in less than a second, which is a pressure change of two atmospheres. If you survive the pounding of one wave, you can be hit by a second one in less than 20 seconds, and then a third can pull you down into what we call a 'triple hold'. Getting held underneath the water by three waves is probably the maximum that a person can take and still survive. I've only known two people who successfully negotiated a triple hold.

Clarke-Jones says, 'You've got to hold your breath and try and curl up into a foetal position. If you stretch out your limbs they can get ripped off by the sheer weight and power of the water, so you try to keep all the parts together. I've broken a couple of ribs,' he adds very matter-of-factly. 'I've dislocated my shoulder, I've broken my back. I landed on my tailbone on a reef, but ... tow-in surfing in deep water is more about dislocating body parts really. The force of those waves can snap your back or rip your arms completely off their hinges.'

Jet ski and helicopter rescue teams have made locating surfers after wipe-outs easier. But it is still hard. In one of the biggest wipe-outs at Jaws, Mike Parsons says he was 'dragged 150 yards underwater'.

POSSIBLE INJURIES

Broken bones. Neck and back injuries. Bruises, gashes and punctures from coral, rocks and surfboards. Drowning.

In 2003 Brazil's Picuruta Salazar rode a single wave for 37 minutes. It was the Pororoca, a large, dirty brown 'bore' or 'eagre' that thunders up the Amazon River during large tidal variations. The Pororoca (the name is said to translate as 'great destructive noise') appears during full moons, can be up to 4 metres in height, and can be heard 15 minutes before it arrives. Salazar braved the piranhas, vampire fish, crocodiles and other local nasties, plus the debris thrown up as the Pororoca creates havoc on the edges of the surrounding jungle. His one ride lasted for 12 kilometres.

Thundering down the Amazon: Picuruta Salazar in 2003.

Photo: Jürgen Skarwan/Red Bull Photofiles

* Jeff Clark. The man who pioneered the rocky, dangerous and altogether humungous Maverick's site off Northern California in 1975. He later recalled: 'As I got closer the sound of the waves breaking was so loud that I could feel them like chills down my spine. That first day I managed to get five waves, barely surviving long enough to kick out of one. [But] it was a great confidence boost for me to have gone where no one had gone before, and to ride waves that were more powerful than anything that I had ever imagined.' Clark soon mastered Mavericks but, amazingly, couldn't find any surfer courageous enough to join him out there for 15 years.

* Greg Noll. A brusque and highly entertaining Californian who was the first modern surfer to conquer Hawaii's Waimea Bay, considered by many to be unrideable. He later said, 'the forbiddingness of the place is what made [it] so compelling.' Noll's fearlessness and intractability earned him the nickname 'Da Bull'. After a powerful storm in 1969 Noll rode a wave at Makaha that is still considered by many to be the largest anyone has ever paddled into.

* Mark Foo. A Singapore-born Hawaiian who drove his car like an ultra-cautious pensioner, yet was so flamboyant on big waves and such an individualistic talent he became a legend in his own short lifetime. Foo's favourite saying was 'If you want to ride the ultimate wave, you have to be willing to pay the ultimate price'. It was thought by some to be merely a self-aggrandising line for the media, but in 1994 Foo paid precisely that price at Maverick's. He disappeared into the blue after an ugly wipe-out, was sucked up to the crest of the wave and then dumped horribly amid thousands of tonnes of white water. His body was found a little over an hour later.

* Ken Bradshaw. The opening scene of the film **Billabong Odyssey** features a Californian named Mike Parsons riding a '64-foot wave'. Spellbinding though that is, it's not the biggest wave ever ridden. By most estimates that was the one caught by Texan Ken Bradshaw on the 'Biggest Wednesday' in 1998. He rode down an 85-foot (25.9-metre) face at Outside Log Cabins off Oahu, Hawaii. He said it looked like a four- or five-storey building moving through the ocean and he thought to himself, 'Oh my God, this is it. This is the one I've been waiting for my whole life.'

South African Andrew Marr hitting the big waves in Hout Bay, Cape Town, South Africa in 2006.

Pretty it's not: Randy Couture demonstrates his hallmark 'ground and pound' style against the face and body of Tito Ortiz in a UFC World Light Heavyweight bout in Nevada, USA.

Photo: Barry Bland/Alamy stock photography

11

MIXED MARTIAL ARTS

OBJECTIVE

To brutalise another competitor by means fair and foul, at least foul by the rules of most other combat sports. Victory in mixed martial arts, or MMA, is achieved by forcing the opponent to 'tap out' (the term for conceding defeat, whether verbally or by tapping on the mat or the opponent's body), or by causing enough damage for the referee or ringside doctor to stop the fight.

REWARDS

Increasingly big purses. Fame or infamy is also assured for anyone who gets to the top of what is seen by many as the most brutal modern sport.

RISKS

Having someone do unto you what you plan to do unto them.

WHY?

Even more than boxing, MMA is a gladiatorial contest, a return to the old days when your sole goal was to fight to the very best of your abilities, unhindered by sanitising rules and regulations.

WHY NOT?

Even more than boxing, MMA is a gladiatorial contest, a return to the old days when your sole goal was to fight to the very best of your abilities, unhindered by sanitising rules and regulations. For many spectators it is just too ugly and too violent. And for many competitors it is hard to get a foothold (or a toelock). One Australian fighter admits that his pay packet for each fight has been less than his medical bills. Furthermore, despite its brutal 'anything goes' ethos, MMA can often consist of two men lying on the canvas locked in positions that look just a bit too Kama Sutric for comfort.

THE RUNDOWN

In ancient times the sport of pankration combined elements of Hellenic boxing and wrestling. There were very few rules, though eye gouging and biting were outlawed, at least in some events. There were no weight categories and no time limit, beyond running out of available light. In such a case there would sometimes be the old-fashioned equivalent of a penalty shootout: the contestants would take turns to deliver undefended blows until one couldn't continue.

While standing, pankration contestants used a variety of strikes with fists, elbows, knees and feet. They also used a series of holds, locks and other wrestling techniques on the ground, which is where most bouts were settled. At any time a contestant could admit defeat by raising the hand or, alternatively, dying.

Permanent injuries and disfiguration were common. Strangulation was the usual cause of death — hence the rush to raise a hand if your opponent formed a winning stranglehold (losing consciousness itself didn't necessarily stop the fight — your opponent was entitled to continue strangling, hitting or twisting). Blows to the head and violent neck twists could also bring about the forfeiture of breathing rights.

Pankration faded with the Greek empire but its spirit was revived, curiously, by a family of Scottish expatriates living in Brazil. In the 1920s, the Gracie brothers, who had been trained in judo by a Japanese neighbour, issued a fighting challenge to all-comers. The challenge was taken up by boxers, wrestlers, karate and jiu-jitsu exponents, kick-boxers and bar-room brawlers, all determined to prove their own technique was superior. It rarely was, because the Gracie brothers had created a very effective hybrid fighting style they called Gracie Jiu-jitsu (others called it Brazilian jiu-jitsu).

Such contests between varied styles of fighters were later known as vale-tudo, Portuguese for 'anything goes'. They became extraordinarily popular in Brazil then spread abroad under different names including 'mixed martial arts'. While this was happening, modern pankration was being born, though with rules more sanitised than those applied in ancient Greece, or indeed in vale-tudo or MMA. So, confusingly, the MMA format is closer to ancient pankration than modern pankration is.

The most famous MMA competition is the Ultimate Fighting Championship or UFC. It was launched in the United States in the early 1990s under the slogan 'There are no rules', and was accompanied by lots of gladiator-style imagery in the publicity. However, perversely, UFC's popularity increased after it introduced rules. These were mostly brought in to make MMA palatable to the American state sanctioning bodies and the cable television stations needed to provide a pay-per-view audience. (Stations that showed early fights quickly distanced themselves from the competition after viewer complaints about the level of violence.) Changes included the introduction of mandatory safety equipment, fingerless gloves and time-limits, and the outlawing of tactics such as head butting, groin strikes, hair pulling and small joint manipulation.

Along the way, the UFC interpretation of the sport has become a huge earner via pay-per-view and DVD sales. It has drawn crowds of over 10 000.

Despite the evolution of UFC from 'there are no rules', to 'there are lots of them', there are still fewer constraints in MMA than in almost any other combat sport. This can be seen in the names attached to various fighting styles: 'ground and pound', 'clinch and pound', 'sprawl and brawl'. Fighters can try to twist their opponent's leg until they pop out a knee, or repeatedly punch someone full in the face while pinning their arms to the ground.

It is rarely elegant (well, when has someone trying to hyperextend someone else's elbow joint been elegant?); equally there can be long and boring clinches that sometimes need to be stopped by the referee for 'inactivity'. The fighting on the mat is highly technical and can be tedious enough to lead to booing. When action occurs, though, it can be quick and spectacular. It can involve moves such as pulling your opponent's face down onto your rising knee—a sort of double blow that can lead to a knockout, or just run-of-the-mill ugly facial injuries.

One common modern rule is that the referee can stop proceedings if a fighter is not 'intelligently defending himself'. It may be hard to think of MMA fighters doing anything intelligently, but many come across as smart and

My personal opinion is that I am not going to be hurt, though in every fight obviously someone is going to be hurt. Whether it is you is dictated by your actions.

It is a really uplifting feeling to strike and feel a person just drop at your feet. Because you put a lot of effort into that strike and to have it connect sweetly ... it's euphoria, like it was meant to be.

articulate. Jon Leven, 34, a former Australian pankration champion and now professional MMA fighter, is one such fighter. He says the appeal is 'the adrenalin rush and the challenge, pitting your skills and your mental application against an opponent's in a fairly real environment.'

Leven doesn't feel any pain during a fight, no matter what happens—'you are running very heavily on adrenalin'—and says he never worries about being hurt.

If you worry about risk of injury I don't think you should be doing a sport that involves injury. My personal opinion is that I am not going to be hurt, though in every fight obviously someone is going to be hurt. Whether it is you is dictated by your actions.

Leven, with a kung-fu background, moved from modern pankration to MMA (in the Welterweight division) because it allows more types of strikes. He prefers cage fighting (where the contestants are effectively locked in) but feels the rules even there should be loosened to allow more things. Leven accepts, however, that tactics such as strikes to the base of the neck should stay banned. 'We are not there to kill each other, we are there to beat the other guy with the best of our abilities.'

Leven says there is an eight-week preparation cycle for the average fight. Yet one of his bouts lasted just 20 seconds—the time it took Leven to knock out Hawaiian champion Coby Jones. And what did that feel like?

*It is a really uplifting feeling to strike and feel a person just drop at your feet.
Because you put a lot of effort into that strike and to have it connect sweetly ...
it's euphoria, like it was meant to be. It's a brilliant feeling. When they are slumped
on the ground, you aren't feeling 'Are they OK?' You are too excited and pumped.
You enjoy the moment ... the crowd is going crazy, and the referee will confirm
the fight win. After that stage you might go and check on him to see if there is any
major damage.*

POSSIBLE INJURIES

Even a winner can expect to spend three or four days being very sore, and
the story can be a lot worse for the loser in MMA. Every type of injury seen
in boxing, kick-boxing, wrestling or almost any other type of contact sport is
commonplace.

'Strikers' use many boxing techniques (as well as those from Asian martial
arts) so MMA fighters are at risk of cumulative brain damage from poundings to
the skull, which can result in the 'punch drunk' syndrome. The 'ground specialists'
cause plenty of twisting and bone-breaking injuries, as winding or stretching your
opponent's limbs until they snap or dislocate is a legitimate tactic. Participating in
MMA isn't good for teeth or long-term good looks either.

Less than a minute into a UFC-sanctioned fight in Las Vegas in 2004, American Frank Mir executed an 'armband submission attempt' on fellow American Tim 'The Maine-iac' Sylvia. It caused the middle of Sylvia's forearm to 'pop' outwards and referee Herb Dean immediately called an end to proceedings. As Sylvia vehemently insisted his arm wasn't broken, Dean argued, equally adamantly, 'I thought I heard it snap, man.' Dean later said that 'it was a strange sound, like maybe somebody ripping some tape or something.' The ringside doctor seemed to agree the arm was broken, but the crowd didn't and Sylvia was determined to continue. Trying to help, Mir said into the microphone, 'Let me break it all the way next time and we won't have this argument. If they want to see me rip it totally off, I'll rip it totally off.' The crowd continued to 'boo' until the big screens showed a close-up replay, at which point the crowd instead went 'yeech'. A later X-ray revealed two breaks in Sylvia's forearm. He didn't fight for several months, returning with a titanium plate in the arm. He went on to regain the UFC Heavyweight Championship belt, which he had relinquished earlier due to the use of anabolic steroids.

* Dioxippus. This famous Athenian was a renowned exponent of pankration. Dioxippus was crowned Olympic champion in 336 BC not through victory but because all the other contenders apparently were too scared to take him on. He was also a close mate of Alexander the Great, demonstrating the esteem in which pankration competitors were once held. Dioxippus once challenged one of Mr Great's most renowned warriors to a stoush and was victorious despite being naked and armed only with a club, while his adversary was dressed in armour and equipped with a spear, sword and javelin.

* Carlos Gracie. A slightly built Brazilian of Scottish ancestry who took out a newspaper advertisement in the mid-1920s saying something to the effect that 'If you want your face smashed or limbs broken, here's where you'll find me'. The so-called Gracie Challenge, essentially an offer to fight any specialist in any fighting style, gave birth to what was known as **vale-tudo** and, later, MMA. The Gracie brothers were hugely successful and took their skills to the United States. In the 1990s, it was Rorion Gracie, son of Helio (and nephew of Carlos), who co-founded the MMA competition known as the Ultimate Fighting Championship.

* Royce Gracie. Rorion Gracie may have helped start the UFC but he left it to his brother Royce to win the first tournament. This contest, in 1993, was hyped as 'the ultimate test to decide what fighting style is superior'. Using the family-developed Brazilian jiu-jitsu, or Gracie Jiu-jitsu as they called it, Royce kept the family's legendary surname in the headlines by following up with victories in the second and fourth UFC competitions, usually by employing grappling techniques against much bigger opponents.

* Randy Couture. A former Graeco-Roman wrestler who became the UFC Heavyweight champion in 2001 with a 'ground and pound' style that involved (in broad terms) forcing an opponent onto his back and raining a variety of different types of blows upon him. Couture, born in Washington, won the UFC Light Heavyweight division at 40 years of age, providing an inspiration for all fighters who were getting on a bit.

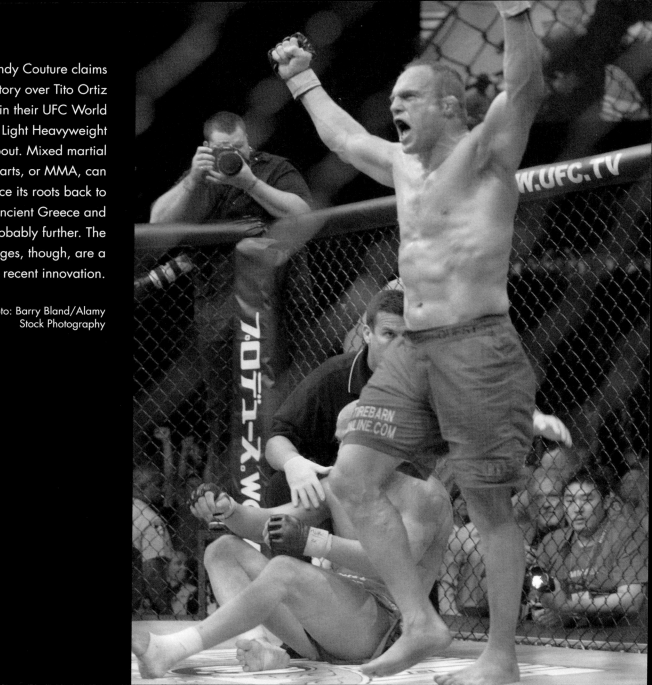

Randy Couture claims victory over Tito Ortiz in their UFC World Light Heavyweight bout. Mixed martial arts, or MMA, can trace its roots back to Ancient Greece and probably further. The cages, though, are a recent innovation.

Photo: Barry Bland/Alamy Stock Photography

The street luges of San Francisco: contestants grab lots of air during a 2002 battle that showed the sport at its maddest and most magnificent.

Photo: Christian Pondella/ Red Bull Photofiles

12

STREET
LUGE

OBJECTIVE

To roll down a long, winding—and very steep—piece of road while lying on an over sized skateboard, and to get to the bottom before the other people rolling down the same hill.

REWARDS

Speed, excitement, the thrill of competition and an opportunity to wear a skintight leather outfit without raising eyebrows among friends and family members. Unfortunately, though, at this time there's little chance of earning a living in the sport, no matter how good you are.

RISKS

Finding out that the board under you … isn't. Even if you manage to stay with your plank on wheels, there's the opportunity to scrape, grate, scour and graze various limbs and bendy bits on the asphalt track. There's speed wobble, too, which can throw you off your board as a prelude to you colliding with any of a broad range of items located between the top of the hill and the bottom. Arrest is also an issue: public liability concerns are such that for many in Australia, the United States and elsewhere, luge practice needs to be done sneakily somewhere at dawn.

WHY?

Street luge offers much of the excitement of motor racing without the accompanying cost, noise, fuel consumption or air pollution. It's easy to learn, fast, furious and spectacular, yet cheaper than almost any other racing conducted on anything other than feet. Piloting a luge on a twisty and challenging course requires athleticism, bravery and mechanical prowess, as the machine can be calibrated to the demands of individual tracks. Interesting new variations such as 'gravity bikes' are broadening the sport's appeal.

WHY NOT?

Exceeding 140 kilometres per hour while lying just centimetres above skin-tearing asphalt, on a glorified skateboard which, under the sport's rules, is strictly prohibited from having a mechanical braking system … are there any other questions? If not, it's worth mentioning that it's tough on footwear. And despite street luge's comparatively high television profile—usually filling those 'How mad are these guys?' segments in sport shows—the number of people competing is very low. Street luge looked ready to burst into the mainstream circa 2000 but it never quite happened. Estimates by Australian and US competition organisers now put it at as few as 30 serious street luge racers in Australia and no more than 1000 worldwide.

THE RUNDOWN

Piloting a traditional luge on snow is fast and often dangerous, but when you replace soft, fluffy white stuff—or even hard-packed ice—with skin-tearing, bone-grinding asphalt and go even faster, well, welcome to street luge.

In the early days, 'gravity racing' was the domain of billycarts or soapbox racers, fitted out with pram or lawn mower wheels, or perhaps ball bearing assemblies. These became increasing sophisticated and achieved remarkable speeds, though mostly in a straight line. In the 1970s skateboarders in southern California created a parallel gravity sport when they started to ride their skateboards while lying in a 'supine' (face up) or 'prone' (face down) position. This greatly increased speeds—and opportunities for mishaps, particularly when riding face down.

The first race was held about 1975 and soon a competition series was being run. This series was held in secret because racing anything on public streets was strictly illegal and, of all the things that could be raced, a tiny vehicle almost invisible to other traffic was probably among the least acceptable.

Modern street luges—ridden feet first and face up—are purpose-built, largely overcoming the problems that occurred when skateboard parts were pressed to travel at much greater speeds than they were designed to (melting wheels was one of the most spectacular). Compared with skateboards, modern luge boards are much longer, with wider axles, up to eight wheels and a lowered section in the centre to ensure the pilot is even closer to the ground. By lying down—sometimes only 2 centimetres above the road surface—the riders reduce their air resistance and increase stability (up to a point). Luge pilots steer by shifting their weight around and still stop, as they always have done, by rubbing their feet on the ground ahead. To help in this regard, some attach strips of car tyres to the soles of their shoes.

Classic street luge, otherwise known as buttboarding, continues to be contested on machines much closer in design to standard skateboards. These have a limit of four wheels, each with a maximum diameter of 70 millimetres. Unlike the early Californians, modern pilots wear proper safety gear including protective suits, gloves and motorcycle helmets.

Speedboards are larger, stand-up skateboards. Riders have adopted streamlined helmets similar to those worn by speed skiers and have stood on these boards at the rather frightening speed of 110 kilometres per hour. The newest branch of the sport involves 'gravity bikes'. These pedal-free two-wheelers run in standard and 'fairing' classes, the latter allowing aerodynamic bodywork that makes them look a little like Grand Prix motorcycles. Speeds of more than130 kilometres per hour have been achieved but, mercifully, gravity bikes have conventional brakes.

The street luge remains the fastest form of the sport, however, and the main centres of activity are the United States, Northern Europe and South Africa. American Tim Cayer competed internationally for five years but a major crash in 2000 put him out of action. He is now the head of Gravity Sport International, which organises competitions, mainly on the east coast of the United States.

For the guys who have that adrenalin itch that needs scratching it is a very inexpensive form of racing. It's much like racing cars or motorcycles. You are riding the line between total control and just a hair-width out.

I went straight into a hay-bale at 60 plus miles per hour. The hay-bale was backed up against a kerb and the only thing that gave way was my knee.

Cayer says the official speed record for luge is about 83 miles per hour (134 kilometres per hour) 'but I know guys who have come very close to the century mark.' That's 100 miles per hour or 161 kilometres per hour. Cayer is sure anyone who has 'the racing blood, that competitive edge' can be a good luge racer.

Most courses are about 1 mile, or about 1.6 kilometres, and races generally take less than two minutes. Like motorcycle racing, luge can involve slipstreaming battles and competitors bumping elbows and knees at very high speeds. Tim Cayer explains:

For the guys who have that adrenalin itch that needs scratching it is a very inexpensive form of racing. And make no doubt about it, it is real racing, it is very competitive … It's much like racing cars or motorcycles. You are riding the line between total control and just a hair-width out. You have to be precise in judgement, thinking ahead constantly, able to visualise the course. Aggressiveness doesn't hurt, by which I mean [pilots] will see an opportunity and they won't second guess themselves, they'll go for it.

Just like motorised racing machines, luges have suspension systems that can be tailored for outright speed or manoeuvrability. If set up too firmly, turning is a problem, if set up too softly, the results can be disastrous at high speed.

'You introduce the potential for a speed wobble,' says Cayer. 'In motorcycle racing they call it a tank-slapper … [it] can be very dangerous as it can spit you right off the board.'

Cayer nominates speedboards as the most dangerous gravity machines—
'they're standing up, so if something goes wrong in front of them, they have the
hardest time avoiding it'—but claims all gravity racing is only as dangerous as
you want to make it. As for his own accident:

> It was in the X-Games qualifier in California. I was leading the pack in my first heat
> and another racer came up and bumped me from behind and I went straight into a
> hay-bale at 60 plus miles per hour. The hay-bale was backed up against a kerb and
> the only thing that gave way was my knee. I broke my knee, broke both my hands,
> had to have surgery to put it all back together. I've still got metal in there now.

So was it worth it taking such risks?

> Sure. That's racing. You believe you are as good or better than the guy next to you,
> that's the challenge. That's what racing is all about.

POSSIBLE INJURIES

Luge pilots enjoy parading their injuries, at least some do on internet message-
boards. Listed wounds run the gamut from 'broken nail' and 'scratched paint'
through to 'drew blood', 'internal bleeding', 'broken bones' and more. Street
luge lends itself to foot and leg injuries, because your feet and legs arrive at
the accident first. Speedboards, where the rider is travelling almost as fast but
standing, adds a much bigger chance of head-butting something unforgiving.
Fatalities in gravity sports, though, are surprisingly rare.

Roland Morrison in full
flight in the Demons of
Downhill—a World Cup
street luge event held in
Bainbridge, Ohio, in 2006.

Photo: Dave Auld,
www.auldovertheroad.com

TRULY
MAD
MOMENTS

Combining the spirit (and speed) of street luge and speedboarding, the flexibility of skateboarding and the madness of motorcycle ramp jumping, in 1999 professional American skateboarder Andy Macdonald claimed a world record by descending a monster slope and jumping his skateboard over four parked cars. The total distance covered was 52 feet 10 inches (16.1 metres). By 2004 this eccentric record had been extended to 79 feet (24.1 metres) by American Danny Way.

163
STREETLUGE

SOME NOTEWORTHY EXPONENTS

* **Darren Lott.** *One of the pioneers of the sport, having started in California in the 1970s and participated in the first (covert) racing series. Lott went on to compete in various forms of gravity racing; in 1998 he was listed in* **The Guinness Book of World Records** *for reaching 65.64 miles per hour (105.64 kilometres per hour) on a standard buttboard.*

* **Pat Brennan.** *One of the few Australian street lugers to have competed overseas, Brennan has also raced from the highest point of the famous Mt Panorama circuit at Bathurst, winding through The Esses and hitting 115 kilometres per hour on Conrod Straight. He later hit 130 kilometres per hour in a competition in Adelaide. 'Huge fun', is his succinct description of that feat.*

* **Roland Morrison.** *A 40-something American who strapped a 100cc Yamaha kart engine to the back of his street luge and took it out to Bonneville Salt Flats, the spiritual home of speed record breaking. He recorded a maximum of 105 miles per hour (169 kilometres per hour) without a hill, but didn't feel it was enough. He is now building a more powerful luge with the aim of hitting 150 miles per hour, or 241 kilometres per hour.*

Opposite: On board in Arizona. This was an 'outlaw' race organised quietly and at short notice in 2003. The 4.5-kilometre track was spiced up by gravel on one high-speed corner and some fairly menacing guardrails.

Photo: Dave Auld, www.auldovertheroad.com

Evel intent: the 19-year-old Lawrence Legend attempts to make his mark. Unfortunately he does. Clearing 15 cars— but not the final ramp— left the young Australian with a shattered ankle but, happily, nothing more serious.

Photo: Lawrence Legend

13

MOTOR
CYCLE
LEAPING

OBJECTIVE

To fly through the air on a motorcycle after leaving a ramp and cover the greatest distance possible. Additional theatrics can include filling the space underneath you with cars, buses or dangerous animals. Riders of the modern freestyle motocross (or FMX) school include loop-the-loops and other moves within their jumps to increase the acrobatic flair and degree of difficulty. To traditionalists, this is mere frippery. Distance is everything.

REWARDS

Fame and the opportunity to make a decent living for an increasing number of FMX performers, thanks to such stunt shows as Crusty Demons and their spin-off DVDs. However, motorcycle jumping has never been as big as it was in the late 1960s and early 1970s, when Evel Knievel was one of the world's most famous people.

RISKS

Missing the landing ramp. Hitting the landing ramp, but while missing your motorcycle. Colliding with anything in between. Arriving at your destination only to have your motorcycle's suspension collapse on impact. Losing control after landing and flying over the handlebars—then being cleaned up by your own machine. According to Stuart Barker's *Life of Evel*, the man born Robert Craig Knievel spent 36 months in hospital during a 15-year jumping career.

WHY?

It's a magnificent contest between man and ... the ground. From a rider's point of view it is, literally, a leap into the unknown; for a spectator it is thrilling and terrifying when a motorcycle is out of its natural element, which is to say high in the air. You can often hear a whole stadium gasping.

WHY NOT?

It's a long preparation period for very short pay-off. Its appeal is not exactly widespread. After a brief heyday on primetime television, it is now often relegated to country shows.

THE RUNDOWN

Motorcycle stunt-riding goes back a long way. America's Louis 'Speedy' Babbs—who broke more than 60 bones in his career—achieved fame by doing loop-the-loops, riding the 'Globe of Death' (speeding around on the inside of a huge barrel) and other stunts from the 1920s onwards. On one occasion,

Babbs raced his motorcycle against a rhesus monkey in a go-kart. When the two collided, the monkey crawled from the wreckage and repeatedly bit Babb's leg.

For many, motorcycle stunt riding came of age in 1967 when Evel Knievel was filmed attempting to jump the fountains at Caesar's Palace Casino in Las Vegas. Knievel crashed on landing, doing an excellent impersonation of a rag-doll in a spin dryer. But when he awoke from a coma, 29 days later, he discovered that he was famous, and the world was transfixed by the idea of men such as him jumping motorcycles over large and inanimate objects.

Unlike most other forms of motorcycle stunt riding, jumping could be measured (either in distance covered or number of cars, buses or semi-trailers over-flown). Evel Knievel jumped 16 cars in one pass in 1967, 18 in 1970 and 19 in 1971. The challenge was on and scores of would-be Evels popped up around the world, leaping their motorcycles to fame or maiming, or perhaps both. A young Englishman who died in 1979 while trying to jump 30 Rolls-Royces was strangely commemorated in the 'Ballad of Robin Winter-Smith', sung by Nanci Griffith.

The advent of more specialised 'motocross' bikes and a bit more science in ramp design eventually made jumping less unpredictable. By then, though, interest was flagging. The 1990s saw a revival, although it centred on freestyle motocross (FMX) jumping, where acrobatic ability was considered the most important element.

The emergence of tricks such as the 'double backflip', 'the backflip no-handed lander', the 'switchblade' and the '360'—any of which would have been considered impossible in Knievel's heyday—also brought a new generation of dramatic wipe-outs, many of them head-first.

Outright distance remained a major challenge for many FMX riders. In late 2005 American Ryan Capes became the first person to break the 300-foot mark, recording a jump of 310.4 feet, or 94.61 metres. 'You actually have to work the bike in the air.' Capes explained later:

Halfway through the jump your bike just wants to fall out from under you. When that happens you really have to stay on top of it and fly the bike. You have to brake and then gas over and over again. I probably hit the brakes and gas four to five times in the air on the 300-foot jump.

The spirit of Evel Knievel still pops up in unlikely places. In July 2005, Iran's local motorcycle hero Javad Palizbanian jumped more than 50 metres across the Karun River. A month later he attempted to leap over 22 buses in Tehran's Azardi Sports stadium, declaring 'I am going to break the world record and do something for my country to be proud of.' Stadium officials insisted that Palizbanian's motorcycle wasn't powerful enough and that the angles of his ramps were all wrong, but he went ahead with the live-to-TV record attempt. He made it only as far as the thirteenth bus and died on impact.

Australia's Lawrence Legend is an old-school motorcycle jumper and, at 35, something of a veteran. Inspired by Evel Knievel, he made his first jump over his mother's car at 14, and in 1999 jumped 11 cars—blindfolded.

'Yes, you need to be a bit mad,' he says, 'but in my case it is genetic. I am the third generation of stunt riders.'

Legend's record, with eyes open, is 20 cars. This involved hitting the ramp at about 120 kilometres per hour, and leaping as high as 14 metres off the ground.

'It will scare the absolute hell out of you beforehand,' Legend says, adding that he never likes to look at the jumps he is attempting from side-on, because it always looks too far.

'But if it is successful, the exhilaration after the event is just a euphoric high.' Which is a way of saying it is more fun to have done it, than to do it?

'Yes, that's the thing,' he responds with a laugh. 'But fear is one of the things

Halfway through the jump your bike just wants to fall out from under you. When that happens you really have to stay on top of it and fly the bike.

It will scare the absolute hell out of you beforehand but if it is successful, the exhilaration after the event is just a euphoric high.

that keeps you alive, that makes you triple check you've done everything right beforehand. You feel sick in the stomach and just wish there were other things.'

Like his hero, Evel Knievel, Legend isn't one for modelling jumps in advance, saying it is all about 'feel'. And people like him tend to feel a lot when they come off:

In my very early stages I fell short of the ramp and the handlebars stabbed me in the stomach and I ruptured my kidneys and was bleeding internally for three days. That slowed me down for a couple of months.

As for the blindfolded jump, he thought it was a good idea until he did it:

It is twice as scary, but it was one of those days that everything went right and I was lucky. I got a call from 'Ripley's Believe It Or Not' who wanted to pay me to do it again for a television show but I said 'No way'.

Lawrence Legend accepts people are watching him with the fascination one reserves for a house burning down, or a road accident.

'They are scared they are going to miss out on something,' he says.

POSSIBLE INJURIES

Severe impact injuries, for a start. There's also bruising, paralysis, puncturing of skin and organs by handlebars, footrests or other parts or the bike, broken bones from collisions with ramps or scenery and, of course, death. Survival is often followed by arthritis and other problems in later life.

In Las Vegas in 1989 Robbie Knievel finally achieved the jump over the fountains at Caesar's Palace Casino that had eluded his father and nearly killed another American jumper, Gary Wells (who missed the side of the landing ramp and went straight into a cement wall, rupturing his aorta and fracturing his pelvis and legs). But as if to say 'so what', in 2006 American freestyle motocross rider Mike Metzger not only jumped over the fountains on live television but performed a mid-air backflip during his 38-metre flight. 'It's something I've wanted to do forever,' said Metzger, who was born in 1975, eight years after Evel Knievel's near fatal Caesar's Palace attempt. Metzger's collection of tattoos includes the word 'Pain' etched inside his mouth—fitting for a man who has broken his back three times, and snaps legs and arms with depressing regularity.

* Evel Knievel.

The original and the maddest. Often wildly under-prepared and using unsuitable equipment (Harley-Davidson road bikes), he grabbed the world's attention when he succeeded—and positively seized it when he didn't. When Knievel jumped 14 Greyhound buses on ABC America's 'Wide World of Sports' in 1975, the television show gained its highest ratings ever with a 52 per cent share. Some of those viewers were possibly, just possibly, hoping he'd fail.

* Dale Buggins.

A youthful Australian daredevil who became a household name in the late 1970s. He broke several records, clearing 25 cars in one jump in 1978, toured the United States and had only one major crash. Buggins took his own life in 1981 shortly before he was due to perform at the Royal Melbourne Show. He was just 20 years old.

* Robby Knievel.

The son of. Although far more accomplished than his dad, he is much less famous. It's all about the timing. In 1999 Knievel Jnr combined triumph and near tragedy when he jumped the Grand Canyon, or at least a small section of it. He leapt over an 800-metre-plus drop on a 500 cc trail bike. He made it to the other side but unfortunately a strong crosswind ensured an Evel rather than a Hollywood ending. Robby missed his landing point and went barrelling over cactuses and hay-bales before being helicoptered, concussed, to a Las Vegas hospital.

* Trigger Gumm.

In May 2005 American Trigger Gumm set an outright world record with an 280-plus feet (84.5-metre) jump at Queensland Raceway. It was a spectacular leap followed by a perfect landing on a large dirt mound. Gumm announced straight afterwards: 'That was mega gnarly, incredible ... insanity at its finest. Everything about it was just danger.' It is believed he was happy. Alas, a year and a bit later, Gumm broke his back while attempting 300 feet (91.4 metres) at a casino in north-east Oklahoma. This left compatriot Ryan Capes to take the '300 foot' honours.

Another day in the office for Lawrence Legend.

Photo: Lawrence Legend

Putting on the spin:
Joey Zuber on his
way down a Kimberley
cliff.

Photo: Mark Watson/Red
Bull Photofiles

14

CLIFF DIVING

OBJECTIVE

To make your way from the top of a very high cliff to water level, unaided, quickly and with a series of graceful manoeuvres.

REWARDS

The satisfaction of having made your way from the top of a very high cliff to water level, unaided, quickly and with a series of graceful manoeuvres. If a modern competitive cliff-diver is very lucky, sponsors may provide a little international travel and spending money, but most need a real job, too.

RISKS

Getting 'lost', which is to say losing your orientation and, as a result, not landing cleanly. Water is not very soft or forgiving when entered from typical cliff-diving heights. According to the Swiss-based World High Diving Federation, 'Making a crash landing into water at 26 metres could be analogised to the same landing on the street at 13 metres'. Even a clean jump subjects the body to enormous forces. At the point of entry into the water, the submerged part of the body is decelerating fiercely while the rest is still accelerating, leaving all sorts of ugly possibilities for compression and unplanned contortion. In a well-organised competition the chances of hitting submerged rocks, which can be fatal, is small. You can still hit fish, however, which can be very, very painful. And in true cliff diving there is the real possibility of hitting the cliff face on the way down, particularly in windy conditions.

WHY?

It has an athletic grace instantly recognisable by any observer, something not always apparent in extreme sports. Nobody has an equipment advantage: it is just the competitor, the cliff, their skill and their bravery (and they need lots of that: the take-off point is high enough that many people wouldn't be game to even stand on it and look over the edge). The divers enjoy almost Formula One

> **Making a crash landing into water at 26 metres could be analogised to the same landing on the street at 13 metres.**

level G-forces, accelerating from zero to 90–95 kilometres per hour in under 3 seconds, then braking with even more fearsome severity: from 95 kilometres per hour back to zero within just three to four metres. Former world champion, Russian Sergey Zotin, once remarked, 'It's not about competition, it is about adrenalin and rush.'

WHY NOT?

The competition is subjective and judged according to a highly complex matrix covering a wide range of scoring manoeuvres. There is not always an obvious winner and both competitors and audience are sometimes unhappy with the results. The safety requirement of having a take-off point 1 metre over the vertical drop line is entirely sensible but it often means the purity of 'cliff diving' is marred by the presence of cantilevered man-made platforms covered in advertising hoardings.

THE RUNDOWN

180
CLIFFDIVING

Like board surfing, cliff diving seems to have its origins in the Hawaiian islands. Legends have it that chiefs would prove their courage by jumping off rocky ledges into the sea. By the early nineteenth century this developed into a more formal sport and hitting the water with the smallest possible splash was considered an important part of any elegant Hawaiian dive (as it still is in most international diving competitions).

There is also a tradition of jumping off the cliffs of La Quebrada in Acapulco, Mexico. The favourite launching points are 27 to 32 metres high, and it was claimed that diving from these represented the only way fishermen could submerge deeply enough to un-snag their nets and lines. It is more likely that it provided a spectacular way of demonstrating machismo on a very small budget.

Either way, when tourism started to build up in Mexico in the 1930s, the leapers of Acapulco discovered there was more to be earned by jumping for tips than for snagged nets. Climbing up cliff faces is dangerous enough, but the Acapulco divers have two extra challenges: first, they need to time their leaps with the tide and incoming waves, otherwise they will hit rock bottom, so to speak. They also risk hitting either the cliff on the way down or the large rocks at the bottom. These rocks stick out as much as 6 metres from the launch sites.

Clips of Acapulco's high divers became a favourite of television sports shows in the United States, Australia and elsewhere in the 1970s and 1980s. This no doubt increased interest in more formal cliff diving competitions. Organisers settled on a range of 23 to 28 metres for diving tournaments, saying beyond that the speeds were so great the danger increased to an unacceptable level.

A typical dive is from 27 metres. The diver hits the water at nearly 100 kilometres per hour and is then pulled up at a rate of deceleration equivalent to that of a mid-level car crash. Early competitions resulted in some broken necks from head-first dives. Diving head-first is still permitted (it carries a bonus 0.6 points for 'degree of difficulty') but the aversion to it felt by most leading divers goes beyond the safety aspect. They feel it is too hard to gain a clean entry into the water.

Most divers instead perform all their complex manoeuvres within the first 10 metres, then finish with a 'Barani' (a front somersault with a half-twist), before landing feet-first.

'Once you are past 10 metres you are generally moving too quickly to have time to fit any more complex manoeuvres,' says 2002 world champion Joey Zuber, from Brisbane, Australia. 'The purpose of the Barani is that you enable

> **There is nothing else that really compares to the feeling of flight with nothing attached to you. When you perform a flying front somersault you watch the water coming towards you ... very quickly I might add.**

It's a good feeling a euphoric feeling, after you've conquered your fears and gone up there and done those difficult dives. Afterwards you are on such a high ... you feel alive.

yourself to land feet-first while still being able to keep your eyes on the water the whole time.'

Zuber says there is 'a tremendous sense of freedom', partly because cliff diving is a sport that requires no equipment:

There is nothing else that really compares to the feeling of flight with nothing attached to you. When you perform a simple dive like a flying front somersault it allows you to feel the acceleration because you watch the water coming towards you ... very quickly I might add.

Before jumping, Zuber tries to visualise the perfect dive in his mind, but it's difficult:

because you've got all these images in your mind of yourself crashing, and you are trying to block out negative thoughts and overcome your fear. Once you take off, you go on auto mode. All those 20 years of training click into place. You are not actually thinking any more ... but you are always making adjustments in the air, and the idea is to try to land as vertically as possible.

As Zuber explained, hitting the water is still a big enough physical shock to make most divers very sore the next day:

You can have a perfect dive and perfect entry, but under the water you've gone sideways. Many people lose a leg, by that I mean the legs are forced apart from the water pressure, with groin tears and worse. People get back problems, neck problems ... When you've done your dive, there's a tremendous sense of relief. You have these two things: shit scared before, and when it is over you feel wonderfully relieved.

So the best part is when it is over?

Yes, in a way. [But] it's a good feeling, a euphoric feeling, after you've conquered your fears and gone up there and done those difficult dives. Afterwards you are on such a high … you feel alive. There is no other way to say it with out sounding cheesy, but it is a rush.

POSSIBLE INJURIES

Broken bones, torn muscles, bruised eyes, blood blisters from the 'slapping' of the water, compression injuries from deceleration, broken neck (if diving head-first), swollen organs and loss of consciousness. In 1999 American diver Todd Michael forgot to insert his mouthguard and almost bit his tongue off on impact. In 2001 *The Washington Post* caught up with 48-year-old Jorge Monico Ramirez, one of the better-known Acapulco cliff divers. It reported 'he has the punctured eardrums and the twisted, sprained shoulders and spine of a man who has made thousands of dives.'

Australian champion diver Joey Zuber performs a forward quarto somersault pike with half twist to win the Red Bull Cliff Diving Lanai title in Hawaii.

Photo: Francois Portmann/ Red Bull Photofiles

Although he was neither competing, nor complying with modern competition rules, German stuntman Harry Arias Froboess deserves a mention in any high diving chronicle. Before moving to Hollywood and jumping, leaping and falling in countless big-budget films, Froboess claimed a world record in 1918 for diving (head-first) a reputed 75 metres from a bridge. Even more spectacularly, in 1936 he was said to have dived 110 metres from a Zeppelin into Lake Constance, though there are no details of whether he landed head- or feet-first—or left in an ambulance. Perhaps Froboess's most remarkable dive wasn't really a dive; it was a 60-metre fall into a river from a collapsing bridge for the 1925 German film *Harry Hills Jagd auf den Tod*. What made it particularly unusual was that he fell with his horse. Froboess escaped serious injury; how his horse fared is less clear.

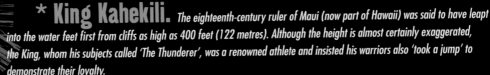

* King Kahekili. *The eighteenth-century ruler of Maui (now part of Hawaii) was said to have leapt into the water feet first from cliffs as high as 400 feet (122 metres). Although the height is almost certainly exaggerated, the King, whom his subjects called 'The Thunderer', was a renowned athlete and insisted his warriors also 'took a jump' to demonstrate their loyalty.*

* Sam Patch. *In 1829 the so-called 'Jersey Jumper' became the first person to dive intentionally over the Horseshoe Falls at Niagara and survive. This and other feats brought the former American cotton-worker enormous fame and inspired books, songs and poems. Patch later stood on a 38-metre platform over a river in Rochester and announced to an 8000-strong crowd: 'Napoleon was a great man and a great general ... but he couldn't jump the Genesee Falls.' Nor, as it turned out, could Patch. He hit the water with a huge and sickening smack and drowned.*

* Frederic Weil. *A Swiss competition diver who still insists on doing it head-first. This gains him extra points for 'degree of difficulty' though, in the words of a competitor, adds an even greater 'degree of stupidity'. During the opening ceremony for the 1998 Cliff Diving World Championship, at Italy's Lake Verbano, Weill performed a 26-metre arm-stand double somersault pike with split and head-first entry—from a helicopter.*

* Orlando Duque. *A Colombian credited with 'the most perfect dive' by the World High Diving Federation. It was achieved during the 2000 world championship in Kaunolu, Hawaii. Duque jumped from 24.4 metres and performed a double back somersault with four twists. He earned ten out of ten from seven out of seven judges.*

* Oliver Favre-Bulle. *In 1987, this Swiss diver executed a double back somersault from 53.90 metres in Villers-le-Lac, France. In doing so he broke the world height record for modern competitive high diving. He also broke his back. In an interview recorded in 2002, Favre-Bulle remarked that 'Every high-dive record holder before me got injured when they tried to set the record as well', as if to say 'that's the price of jumping from that high up'.*

Historic jump: A multiple exposure of Joey Zuber launching off the Old Bridge in Mostar, Bosnia-Herzegovina, and landing with scarcely a splash.

Photo: Samo Vidic/Red Bull Photofiles

Harry Egger—with aerodynamically enhanced rear-end—during a speed run in Portillo, Chile. On his sponsor's website, Egger lists his personal philosophy as: 'only dead fishes are swimming with the current'.

Photo: Bernhard Spöttel/
Red Bull Photofiles

15

SPEED SKIING

OBJECTIVE

To achieve the highest outright speed on snow skis, and safely slow to a stop, while wearing a huge aero-helmet that makes you look a little like an interstellar bug.

REWARDS

There's not much money in it, but plenty of excitement for participants and spectators, also the potential for inclusion in *The Guinness Book of World Records* as the fastest non-motorised sportsperson on land.

RISKS

Coming off your skis, either by aerodynamic instability, hitting a bump or making a mistake. Failing to keep your legs together at 250 kilometres per hour, which … no, let's stop there.

WHY?

It allows people to travel on land faster than most sky divers achieve in freefall. (In a standard belly-to-ground position, sky divers usually top out at 192 to 200 kilometres per hour before popping their 'chutes.) The stakes are high, everything happens at the very edge of human and mechanical limits and it's breathtaking to watch. It is also great to listen to. Speed skiers produce one of the most wonderful fighter-plane-like 'whooshes' in sport.

WHY NOT?

You need expensive and highly specialised equipment, plus wind-tunnel research if you want to be at the pointy end of the field. Speed skiing also requires snow, and even when you've got that there is a limited number of places where the sport can be practised. There is no head-to-head competition and one run can look much the same as the next with only the timing equipment revealing the winner.

THE RUNDOWN

There are not many sports in which the object is to crouch down and keep perfectly still, but that is the only way in which you are going to be competitive in this spectacular, and spectacularly unpredictable, form of skiing. The human body is not a particularly aerodynamically efficient shape and no other land sport exposes it to the wind at such speeds (motorcycle racers have fairings to cope with the air turbulence).

One academic paper, 'Aerodynamics of speed skiers' (Thompson, Friess and Knapp II, 2001), claims that aerodynamic loads constitute more than 80 per cent of the total drag during the fastest part of the run. The 'tuck' adopted by speed skiers is designed to present as small an area as possible to the wind because the less of it you catch, the faster you go. That's also the reason for the oversized aerodynamic helmets and streamlined suits with slippery rubber surfaces. The skiers' legs are often covered with wing-like enclosures, with vortex generators to try to stop them being pushed out of line.

Even the ski poles are special, low-drag units that wrap around the skier's body. Every shape is smoothed to cheat the wind. When he hit 248.28 kilometres per hour in 2002, Austrian Harry Egger wore a long, pointed tail. Aerodynamicists had discovered his derrière was not very efficient through the air-ière.

The quest to be the fastest person on skis is nothing new. Most lists of world skiing records start with Gustav Lantschner, an Austrian who hit 105.7 kilometres per hour in St Moritz in 1930. The 150 kilometres per hour barrier was broken soon after World War Two but it wasn't until 1982 that anyone achieved 200 kilometres per hour. That was American Steve McKinney, who was greatly aided by continuing improvements in research, materials and track preparation (as well as his own skill and bravery).

In 1992 speed skiing appeared in the Winter Olympics as a demonstration sport; it attracted huge interest but, unfortunately, Switzerland's Nicolas Bochatay was killed when he hit a snowmobile during a practice run on a nearby public slope.

Three years later Jeff Hamilton broke the 240 kilometres per hour barrier, though as a Californian, he saw his achievement more as surpassing the 150 miles per hour mark. Hamilton explained that the task was to stay motionless in exactly the right pose while 'the wind is trying to rip you apart'.

Other Europeans and Americans clawed an extra kilometres per hour or two until 2002, when the 250 kilometres per hour barrier was finally eclipsed by Frenchman Philippe Goitschel.

Speed skiing meetings can last several days. The first runs usually start halfway up the hill and the competitors move up in increments. In the final phase they are sliding down from the very top of hills that look more like the sides of skyscrapers. Speed skiers can reach 160 kilometres per hour after just five seconds and 200 kilometres per hour within 10 seconds.

The trip is hardly smooth. Spectators can see the 2.4 metre-long skis lifting off the ground, the skier's legs shaking violently, the skier's body looking impossibly frail beneath the huge helmet. Franz Weber, Austria's multiple speed skiing world champion, explained to an American television audience what it is like from the other perspective:

> At about 120 to 125 miles per hour [193 to 201 kilometres per hour] you start to experience very violent vibrations but if you are brave enough or crazy enough, whichever you want to call it, you get to the point that the wind pressure on your ski tips becomes so strong you start to take off the ground and actually go on a cushion of air … this sensation is very strange because you actually feel a lot smoother and feel like you are going a lot slower … basically I call it the sound barrier, the Mach 1, on skis.

Speed skiing is very technical, with many competitors spending over two hours each competition day waxing their skis both to reduce friction and to best match their skis to the changing condition of the snow. Australian champion Michael Milton says: 'I keep about 20 different types of wax in my kit. I combine and layer them, depending on a range of temperatures through the day.'

Speed skiers can wax more than their skis. They can wax lyrical about snow crystal shape, the quantity of free water in the surface, aerodynamic stability

You get to the point that the wind pressure on your ski tips becomes so strong you start to take off the ground and actually go on a cushion of air.

We deal with risks every day of our lives. I'm not going to live in a cave to avoid them.

considerations and drag coefficients. A course is quickest when the temperature is rising and there is a thin film of water on the surface.

'The track is the engine that pushes you,' says Milton. 'All you do is try to use that engine as efficiently as possible.' Some days are very fast, he says, others are not.

If a speed skier manages to stay upright on the way down, the next challenge is stopping. Because all the aerodynamics are designed for the standard tuck position, everything can go haywire when the skier moves out of this position.

To stop, the skier gradually raises their body and spreads their arms but it is very easy to become unsettled, or even to be pushed onto their back. If a competitor were to stand up quickly the wind pressure would rip him or her clean out of the bindings.

Since 2002, several people have broken 250 kilometres per hour (three in one competition in 2006, for example), but none by very much. The world record is held by Italy's Simone Origone, who hit 251.4 kilometres per hour at Les Arcs in France. The woman's record is only slightly slower: in April 2006 Sweden's Sanna Tidstrand recorded 242.59 kilometres per hour.

New Yorker Tracie Max Sachs has achieved 238 kilometres per hour or, as she puts it, 'the speed a lot of big jets land at.' She adds 'The vibration is definitely big. Jets land on a flat surface, but imagine on a ski track that has been used 30 times before you. It should be perfect, but it rarely is.'

Max Sachs says her technique is to focus on keeping the skis flat and staying tightly in the tuck position, no matter what happens:

At Les Arcs your skis skip on the surface of the snow when you go above 200. The sensation is that basically you are between skiing and flying, you're trying to hold your position but you are leaving the ground a bit, you are getting lift under your body ... and in the air is not fast.

She says 'a huge factor of speed skiing is the mental':

> You have to have the confidence, the stability and the mental focus to do these runs, even though they are very short, mentally they are very long. If you are in a tuck position for 30 seconds and imagine yourself bobbing up and down and dealing with side winds and head winds, there are a lot of factors you have to deal with ... you can get pushed around a lot.

And is it exciting? 'The rush really is afterward,' she says. 'You are so focused on so many things during the run and prior to the run and when you come down and see your result, that's when the elation comes in.'

Max Sachs has crashed several times. Once she fell at 212 kilometres per hour and was concussed, on another occasion she hit a compression at the bottom of the track:

> I got sucked into it and broke my coccyx bone in three places. That was extremely painful. Having a concussion is nothing in comparison to breaking your ass. Still, I don't see there being much more risk than in any other extreme sport. We deal with risks every day of our lives. I'm not going to live in a cave to avoid them.

Although men are achieving higher speeds, probably because they are stronger and can hold themselves more still, small women present a lower frontal area and are therefore more efficient through the air. It is possible they could catch up.

POSSIBLE INJURIES

There have been no fatalities recorded during official speed skiing competitions, mainly because the tracks are built well away from trees and fences. However there have been many impact injuries, broken bones and burns. Snow turns to fire when you are sliding along it at autobahn cruising speeds. Harry Egger once described it as 'burning everywhere. So you first go on your back and then you go on your hand and you're like a sausage. You're like a sausage on a barbeque.'

Wind tunnel testing is a necessity for speed skiers to gain those last few kilometres per hour. Here Tracie Max Sachs faces her biggest fan.

Photo: Phillipe May

In 1997 Jeff Hamilton survived the fastest crash in the history of non-motorised land sport: 243 kilometres per hour, or 151 miles per hour. One of the benefits of the slippery suits used in speed skiing is that they ensure the skier slides rather than tumbles. As a result, the American fractured only three minor bones. The downside of sliding is that Hamilton was badly burned all over his body. He told 'CBS News' shortly afterwards: 'I crashed for six football fields, six football fields sliding. That first football field happens in two seconds. It feels like being in a frying pan and being hit with a baseball bat at the same time.'

SPEEDSKIING

* Philippe Goitschel. The man who, in 2002, finally broke the 250 kilometres per hour barrier. The 40-year-old French ski champion and golf instructor achieved 250.7 kilometres per hour down a specially prepared track at Les Arcs in the French Alps. 'Considering the human being, the equipment, we have known for a long time that we could reach the speed of 250 kilometres per hour,' he declared. 'This morning we had favourable parameters, an excellent ski run and a very good weather.' As for technique, Goitschel said, 'The main thing is to win over the skis which tend to go everywhere at those speeds.'

* Harry Egger. An Austrian who has set many speed records but was pipped at the post for the 250 mark. He believes the way to go better again is to head for the Himalayas, where the air is not so thick. Egger is planning a speed record attempt there and believes he can hit as much as 275 kilometres per hour.

* Michael Milton. When this Australian hit 213.65 kilometres per hour in France in 2006 it made him not just the fastest Australian in outright terms, but the fastest one-legged skier in the world. Milton is a multiple Paralympic gold medal winner in other skiing disciplines and came to speed skiing only in 2003. His Australian record was 1.4 kilometres per hour faster than the speed achieved by the able-bodied Nick Kirschner in 1997 and is one of the few times an athlete with a disability has held an open record. Theoretically, Milton's body has less air drag, but he can't bend as low or put his chest between his knees as most other skiers do. It's far more difficult for him to achieve stability and he has to twist his torso and bring his right arm forward so that he can compensate for the uneven pressure of the wind on his body. 'Speed skiing,' Milton says, 'is about balance, aerodynamics and overcoming fear.'

Fire and ice: Tracie
Max Sachs hits 238.57
kilometres per hour in
Les Arcs, France.

Photo: Jenny Milton

Just one of those crazy flings: the Dangerous Sports Club's extraordinary trebuchet in action.

Photo: Bill Fryer

16

TRE
BUCH
ET

OBJECTIVE

To fly through the air, propelled by a massive trebuchet (a counterweighted catapult equipped with a sling to increase launch speed and distance), then land safely in a large net.

REWARDS

Surviving. Enjoying rapid acceleration and three to four seconds of human flight. Bragging about it later.

RISKS

Not surviving. Missing the net, hitting the net but bouncing out of it, hitting the net but twisting or breaking something on impact.

WHY?

It amply fulfils the brief of such eccentric organisations as the Dangerous Sports Club and the later Oxford Stunt Factory, by being 'innovative, exciting and perilous'. Claims are also made for it being an art-form and an important demonstration of the right of the individual to take risks if he or she are the only likely victim.

WHY NOT?

Once you've seen one person flung through the air by a trebuchet, you've probably seen them all. More importantly, the person flying through the air has little control over where they land, rather compromising any ability to get better with practice. People who insist trebuchet is a dangerous sport may be only half correct.

THE RUNDOWN

The modern trebuchet came to international prominence only through tragedy. In 2002, 'Dino' Yankov, a 19-year-old Bulgarian student, joined the Oxford Stunt Factory and paid £40 to be flung by a trebuchet across a clearing behind a car park in Somerset, England.

The trebuchet is best known as a medieval siege engine. It uses a counterweight and a lever arm with sling to propel objects a great distance and with enormous force. In the time of knights and armour, trebuchets flung large rocks at—and sometimes through—castle walls from as far as a third of a kilometre away. They could be used to fire humans back then, too, usually dead plague victims, who were flung over the castle walls in the hope of spreading the disease.

Yankov covered about 30 metres at up to 88 kilometres per hour but missed the safety net and died that night. Eight days later the trebuchet makers, David Aitkenhead and Richard Wicks, were arrested and charged with manslaughter.

David Aitkenhead was a mid-1980s recruit to the Dangerous Sports Club (DSC), a rather eccentric group of past and present students from Oxford University who had invented bungee jumping in 1979, skateboarded with the bulls in Pamplona and had sent a grand piano down the Saint Moritz ski slopes (one member steering, another playing Chopin). Aitkenhead became the DSC's human catapult specialist and the Oxford Stunt Factory, a later and more commercially astute organisation, used his services at some of its gatherings.

Aitkenhead and Wicks were acquitted of the manslaughter charge in what DSC president David Kirke described as 'an extraordinary test case, about the right to experiment, at personal risk, versus social responsibility.'

Kirke had always been a fan of the trebuchet, celebrating his 55th birthday by being flung. He rejected a crash helmet in favour of a stylish beret:

> It starts slow, or seems to, then really whips you along. It is like being whooshed into some sort of vortex or wind tunnel. It is very exciting, very powerful. The only analogy I can think of is when you see those strange sci-fi type movies and you are spiralling into a hollow in space. You are going very, very fast and at one stage I thought I had completely lost it and I was going to land beside the net, but that was just the effect of being spiralled.

Aitkenhead and Wicks's human trebuchet—the best known, but far from the only one in existence—flings people at a height of more than 20 metres and, depending on their weight, they reach nearly 90 kilometres per hour at the fastest point. And the landing? 'Not too bad at all,' claims Kirke:

Hand in front of face, elbows by side, etc. ... you tend not to break your neck by twisting—it is sideways movement of the head. Various precautions like that. There is a second net underneath to help take up the stress and you whiz back about 10 to 15 feet in the air and it is a nice bouncy feeling.

Kirke says of the trebuchet 'it represents a new way of travelling through the air for fun and pleasure and interest,' and the court case should never have happened. 'If it is experimental, if the risks are pointed out and they sign a written disclaimer, then it's nobody else's business.'

Kirke has been an advocate of taking risks since the DSC was formed in the late 1970s, on the proviso he says, that the risk 'is for an innovation that may inspire or be interesting.' In that spirit, he was the was first person in the world to bungee jump, leaping off the Clifton Suspension Bridge over the River Avon while wearing a top hat and the DSC's official necktie, depicting a silver wheelchair with a blood red seat. Kirke was carrying a bottle of champagne at the time but it slipped from his hand at the bottom of the drop as he was whipped back skyward: 'I was a complete idiot and should have had it strapped to my wrist ... because I lost my breakfast.'

Although the Oxford Stunt Factory trebuchet fell into disuse while the court case was on, there are people planning to reenergise the sport—or activity. Kirke likens flinging people with the trebuchet to a work of art and defends the safety record by mentioning that nine people a year die playing cricket.

'The highest cause of skiing accidents in America is fat middle-aged gentlemen who fall asleep after lunch while on skis, having drunk too much.'

POSSIBLE INJURIES

Broken bones, skin abrasions from colliding with the safety net and, in at least one case, death.

It represents a new way of travelling through the air for fun and pleasure and interest.

The trebuchet is but one of various machines designed to fling people into the air. In the late 1980s, members of the Dangerous Sports Club built a Roman-style catapult. Soon afterwards, they acquired a device designed to launch target drones off the sides of warships and immediately used it to fire their president, David Kirke, off a rocky strip of Irish coastline. The violence of the acceleration was so great it caused Kirke major back injuries, and he came very close to colliding with the cliffs after popping his parachute. Still, he said it was 'enormous fun and terrific, and there were great celebrations afterwards.'

207
TREBUCHET

* Dean Dunbar. *A modern English adventurer whose response to deteriorating eye-sight was to quit his job and race around the world trying every manner of extreme activity he could. Although legally defined as blind, Dunbar has sampled sky diving, hang gliding, white water rafting, helicopter bungee jumping and the trebuchet: 'Before I knew it, I was airborne,' he reports in his adventure logbook (www.extremedreams.co.uk). 'The action was surprisingly smooth. I was in the air for 3 to 4 seconds ... I did a couple of somersaults before I hit the net. The landing was a little heavy and I realised that a pair of thick gloves may have been a good idea. But if a slightly grazed wrist was my only injury, I could hardly complain.'*

* Graham Chapman. *The Monty Python team member was a big fan of the Dangerous Sports Club and although he didn't live to experience its trebuchet, he was earlier slung into the air for charity in what could best be described as a reverse bungee jump. Members of the DSC placed Chapman in a harness, which was attached to a bungee rope, which in turn was tied to a crane. Chapman was clamped the ground while the crane was lifted to maximum height, fully stretching the rope. When the clamps were released, Chapman was hurled skywards with a force of 6G. He later summarised the flight in one word: 'ZIIIIINNNNNGGGG!!!'*

* Stella Young. *The third person to try the 'human trebuchet' built by David Aitkenhead and Richard Wicks, and the first to be injured. In 2000 she bounced off the net onto the ground and broke her pelvis in three places. The muddy ground cushioned her fall and may have saved her life, though it hampered the ambulance that came to pick her up. Young gave evidence at the inquest into 'Dino' Yankov's death on the same trebuchet, saying she had warned him: 'It is a very, very dangerous thing to do.'*

* Ron L. Toms. *An American who used a self-designed and built trebuchet to fire himself, and later several friends, into the Blanco River in Texas during the 1990s. 'When I hit the water, I was elated!' he later wrote. 'My dream of riding an ancient throwing machine had come true! I came up laughing.'*

David Kirke, the first man in the world to bungee jump, prepares to experience a far more powerful force. Moments later he was launched through the air by trebuchet to celebrate his 55th birthday.

Photo: Bill Fryer

The fastest Australian on land, ever: Rosco McGlashan en route to exceeding 1000 kilometres per hour in *Aussie Invader 3* at Lake Eyre. Next target: 1000 miles per hour—or more than 1600 kilometres per hour.

Photo: Richard Humphrys Photography

17

LAND SPEED RECORD BREAKING

OBJECTIVE

To achieve the highest possible speed
in a vehicle with wheels, while in full
contact with the ground, and live to talk
about it. The International rules say a
run must be performed over a measured
mile in two directions within an hour.
This negates any advantages of wind
or gradient, and tends to disqualify a
vehicle that blows itself to pieces in the
attempt and sprays its bits over the
finish line.

REWARDS

Moderate fame, but no riches. There is no prize for setting a land speed record, or LSR. Craig Breedlove claimed to have put US$1.5 million into his unsuccessful 1996/97 attempt while Britain's sound-barrier breaking *Thrust SSC* was such a shoestring effort it contained some second-hand parts from the car that set the land speed record 14 years earlier.

RISKS

You can't really test what will happen when you drive a vehicle faster than anyone has ever driven a vehicle before. And sometimes things go wrong well before you are anywhere near the record. Many have died in the attempt to be the fastest person on land, and breaking the sound barrier now adds a whole new level of danger, as at ground level the shock waves are unpredictable.

WHY?

It is a huge technical challenge to produce a car that travels almost as fast as a speeding bullet. (A typical rimfire .22 rifle fires at about 1300 to 1400 kilometres per hour, about 10 per cent faster than the current land speed record.) Driving such a vehicle takes enormous bravery and concentration; when you are covering a kilometre every three seconds, the slightest hesitation can cause everything to be lost.

WHY NOT?

It's ludicrously expensive, of limited appeal and needs to be a done a long way from anywhere you'd want to go. Salt lakes, chosen because they are very large, flat, dry and featureless are, for precisely the same reasons, not good places to spend the days and sometimes months it takes for the right conditions to arrive. And by some accounts, driving an LSR machine isn't even fun.

THE RUNDOWN

In the early days of the LSR there were electric and steam-powered contenders, but the contest was soon dominated by people shoving enormous airplane engines into road cars. Such monstrous powerplants made for automobiles that were very quick, extremely unpredictable and daftly dangerous. Furthermore, record runs were often conducted on public roads, beaches and other highly unsuitable venues.

Welshman J.G. Parry Thomas used a gargantuan 27-litre engine in the LSR special known as 'Babs' and in 1926 he reached 275.3 kilometres per hour. The next year he attempted to go even faster on the seven-mile Welsh beach known as Pendine Sands. Unfortunately, the huge engine blocked Thomas's vision and required him to lean to the right to be able to see ahead. This placed his head directly above one of the two chains taking power to the rear wheels. At about 270 kilometres per hour, the chain broke, partially decapitating the driver, sending the car into a roll and precipitating a fireball.

Others died chasing the LSR, but the speeds rose dramatically, reaching 484.6 kilometres per hour by 1935 and nearly 600 kilometres per hour by the advent of World War Two.

Donald Campbell's 648.73 kilometres per hour, achieved in 1964 on Australia's Lake Eyre, was really the last hurrah for wheel-driven cars. After that, the rules were changed and jets, rockets and even Sidewinder missiles provided the motive power for successful 'outright' record attempts.

The second half of the 1960s saw the record continually being attacked and beaten, and additional drivers perishing. In 1970 the 1000 kilometres per hour benchmark was passed. All that seemed left to do was to break the speed of sound on land (it had been broken in the air for the first time in 1947), but suddenly things went quiet.

It wasn't until 1983 that Richard Noble broke the 1970 record by reaching 1020 kilometres per hour and the speed of sound wouldn't officially be surpassed until the 1990s. Australia's Rosco McGlashan announced an ambitious challenge at the start of the decade, but it soon became clear the 'speed of sound' shoot-out would come down to two drivers: 1960s' veteran Craig Breedlove in the third version of his Spirit of America jet-car, and the much younger British fighter pilot Andy Green in the twin-jet *Thrust SSC*.

In 1996, Breedlove turned up at Black Rock Desert, Nevada, ready to break Richard Noble's record, still standing after 13 years. After being told on the radio that the crosswind was 'one five', which Breedlove took to mean a quite manageable 1.5 knots, he blasted across the desert only to be hit by a crosswind much closer to the 15 knots the radio message had intended to convey. While travelling at a speed estimated to be 1080 kilometres per hour, Breedlove noticed from his tiny cockpit in the nose that the right side of his car was lifting. In a blinding cloud of dust, the car took a violent turn and narrowly missed a spectator area as it tilted, threatened to tip and generally did its best to shake itself to pieces.

A very groggy Breedlove managed to walk away from the world's fastest car accident but the car needed rebuilding, and *Thrust SSC* was ready for its assault.

Thrust SSC was in many ways a brutal instrument (it weighed 10 tonnes and had rear-wheel steering) and was as ugly as Breedlove's car was graceful. Yet with Andy Green at the controls it was the car that produced an unmistakeable sonic boom twice within an hour, recording an average speed for the two runs of 1227.952 kilometres per hour and finally taking the LSR above the speed of sound.

Wing commander Andy Green says the hardest thing about driving a record-breaking car is that you can't practice the way you would in a racing car. 'Pretty much every time is your first time because you are changing things. It's a developmental vehicle with very little to no running experience.'

Green eventually completed 14 runs above 700 miles per hour (1127 kilometres per hour), 'inching up through the transonic region', as he puts it, to study the changing shock waves:

The majority of the world's experts on the subject said this is impossible, the shock waves will go unstable and the car will be destroyed.

The heart pounds pretty quickly once you light the wick and go.

The majority of the world's experts on the subject said this is impossible, the shock waves will go unstable and the car will be destroyed. We found a way of managing that process for the first time and that was the key.

The shock waves couldn't be felt when the car went supersonic but Green could certainly hear them. 'They were very loud over a carbon fibre cockpit with no sound deadening.'

Green, who talks almost as quickly as he drives, makes the process sound clinical and undramatic, though he does admit 'there was quite a bit going on in the cockpit' as he accelerated from 320 kilometres per hour to 1000 kilometres per hour in about 20 seconds.

The rear-wheel steering, chosen for stability reasons, made the car horrible to handle. At times *Thrust SSC* was slewing around so much Green had to apply 90 degrees of steering lock to keep the thing something close to on line. 'After a year of practising I could just about drive it most of the time,' he said.

When asked if setting the LSR was fun, Green's reply was a simple 'No.' He said there was too much pressure at the time, not helped when a press photographer was paid a retainer specifically to record the massive accident so many expected. 'Only months later ... you can sit back and start to enjoy it.' Despite everything, Green argues it was not dangerous:

I live in Central London. I'm far more likely to be hit by a bus ... if something goes wrong in the LSR it's massively more spectacular of course, but you are still dead. Over 15 per cent of all the people who have been up Everest are still up there. With the land speed record, despite the most ridiculous lack of safety at times ... they've only managed to kill about 2 per cent of all the people who have ever attempted it.

In October 2006 Breedlove's car was sold second-hand—low mileage, one owner, minor accident damage fully repaired. The buyer was tycoon adventurer

Steve Fosset, who plans to use it to beat Green's record. The only Australian to exceed 1000 kilometres per hour on land is the quietly-spoken Rosco McGlashan. He is currently working on *Aussie Invader 5R* in preparation for an autumn 2008 LSR assault, and says computer modelling shows the new rocket-powered car will exceed 1000 miles per hour (1609 kilometres per hour). 'It's been a lifetime ambition,' McGlashan says:

> *Donald Campbell came across to Lake Eyre in 1964. I was 12 and I said to my mates 'That was pretty good but I can go a lot quicker than that'. And I left school about a week later and went off to achieve my dream. I've been working seven days a week and seven nights a week ever since. A bit mad? Yeah, I suppose it is an obsession.*

In all his record breaking, which includes drag racing and driving a rocket-powered go-kart at 407 kilometres per hour, McGlashan says he has escaped major injuries. 'I've broken a few bones, wore a bit of skin off here and there, but nothing super serious.' The fastest McGlashan has achieved is 1026 kilometres per hour, averaged through the measured mile in 2002, but he couldn't make a return run. This was on a 150-kilometre course marked out on Lake Eyre, South Australia:

> *The place is so flat and so long when you accelerate in the car you are looking over the curvature of the Earth. You've got a marker barrel every kilometre—and each of those disappears in about 4 seconds—and as we are running along the track I'm sort of lifting my bum out of the seat trying to look over the hill, if you like. It looks like a short, steep hill.*

He says, in his understated way, that 'the heart pounds pretty quickly once you light the wick and go.' McGlashan continues: 'I wouldn't say it is fun, you do say to yourself "What am I doing here, what is this all about?" What dominates my mind is "I need to achieve to set a record, and not stuff up".'

POSSIBLE INJURIES

Severe impact injuries, death, burning from exotic fuels, inhalations, vibrations, conflagrations. Even if having a crash doesn't break anything (or everything), bruising can come with the terrain even in a successful run. The shaking, shuddering and juddering are often extreme.

The fastest car in history—*Thrust SSC*—in the Desert Pits.

Photo: SSC Programme Ltd

Although the record books say Andy Green was the first man to break the speed of sound on land, stuntman Stan Barrett claims to have done so 18 years earlier in his 12-metre long, needle-thin, rocket-powered *Budweiser* three-wheeler. The most remarkable thing about Barrett's 1979 run was that, when he reached approximately 1000 kilometres per hour, he lit a secondary power source—a 12 900 horsepower Sidewinder missile. Barrett recalled that at that moment he fitted in just one word: 'wow'. With the Sidewinder in play, the rear wheels lifted clean off the ground, leaving the vehicle running on its single nose wheel. The top speed for the run was claimed as 739.666 miles per hour (1190.38 kilometres per hour, or Mach 1.0106). Unfortunately, the speed was not measured according to international standards nor, as specified by record rules, was a second run completed, nor was there an audible sonic boom. What is not in dispute, though, is that the vehicle went very bloody quickly and that Barrett was as brave as LSR contestants come. 'I wasn't afraid of getting hurt, and I certainly wasn't afraid of dying,' he later said. 'I was as prepared to die as I was to live.'

* **Donald Campbell.** *A highly superstitious Englishman, who always drove in the company of his teddy bear, Mr Whoppit. Campbell named his record-breaking cars and boats Bluebird, in honour of his father, Sir Malcolm, who had done likewise. (Malcolm Campbell was the first to drive a car at 300 miles per hour.) Donald Campbell set world records on land and water in Australia in 1964 but died trying to better his water speed record in England three years later. His last words were captured on the boat's radio: 'I can't see anything ... I've got the bows up ... I've gone ... oh ...' Mr Whoppit's body was recovered soon afterwards, but Campbell's remains (and those of his boat) lay at the bottom of Coniston Water until 2001.*

* **Craig Breedlove.** *The man who, in his **Spirit of America** jet cars, who was the first to break the 400, 500 and 600 miles per hour barriers, which equate to the slightly less rounded 643, 804 and 965 kilometres per hour marks. In 1964 Breedlove lost a parachute that was meant to slow him down, skidded for ten kilometres, knocked over two telegraph poles and smashed into a lake at nearly 800 kilometres per hour. When rescuers arrived he mumbled: 'For my next trick, I'll set myself on fire'. In late 2006 Breedlove was still talking about a comeback but he failed to secure a sponsorship deal for a new attempt and announced his retirement shortly afterwards.*

* **Gary Gabelich.** *An American who turned to drag racing when he failed to make the US astronaut programme. Gabelich was the man who first exceeded 1000 kilometres per hour on land, in the rocket-powered **The Blue Flame** in 1970. Before each high-speed run, the love bead-carrying Gabelich would stroke the nose of his machine and say things such as 'Let's do it together baby ... give me a good ride. Let's go and do our thing together, baby, you and me.' **The Blue Flame** obviously liked such talk, putting in a near faultless performance. Gabelich was reportedly planning a supersonic record attempt 14 years later when his speeding motorcycle collided with a truck on a public road in California. A man who had survived 1000 kilometres per hour on the salt hadn't thought it necessary to wear a helmet on the road and died in hospital three hours later. He was 43 years old.*

* **Andy Green.** *The Brit who is officially the fastest man on land, thanks to his efforts in **Thrust SSC**. He remains the only driver to set a supersonic land speed record. **Thrust SSC** was actually flying at times and shaking itself to bits, but in-car footage shows the ice-cool Green coolly counting off the speedo: '400 miles per hour, 500 miles per hour, 600 miles per hour ...' LSR competitor Rosco McGlashan says that 'Andy Green is the only guy who could ever have driven that SSC car. It was an absolute pig. It was the worst-engineered car that has ever tried for a land speed record.'*

Thrust SSC entering the measured mile at Black Rock Desert, Nevada USA, in the first of the two runs that set the first and only 'supersonic' land speed record. Note the shock waves above the vehicle. The year was 1997.

Photo: SSC Programme Ltd

Double freefall:
the age-old dream
of drifting through
clouds is now just an
aeroplane ride—and a
leap through an open
door—away.

18

SKY
DIVING

OBJECTIVE

To throw yourself from an aircraft, perform any number of exciting or interesting manoeuvres, stunts or gymnastic routines in the space between heaven and earth, then land smoothly and safely.

REWARDS

The freedom of flight: modern 'chutes are, effectively, self-inflating wings so it's not just falling out of the sky with the brakes on, as it was in the old days. It really feels like flying and high forward speeds are possible, as are turns, twists and swoops. Sky divers also enjoy a feeling of superiority: they call non-sky divers 'Whuffos' (as in 'Whuffo you jump out of a plane?'). They insist it is not a derisive term, but they are not to be believed.

RISKS

Aaahhhh … splat!

WHY?

The thrill of speed (more than 500 kilometres per hour is possible) and not having to rely on any motor, other than the one that got you up into the air in the first place. It's extremely diverse (ranging from sky surfing to wingsuit flying to speed sky diving) and surprisingly inclusive (read *Skydiving with Wheelchair Persons* by Australian Paul Murphy).

WHY NOT?

Any sport that requires an aircraft is going to be expensive and unwieldy. Direct head-to-head competition is difficult; most branches of the sport are judged according to highly subjective criteria. And yes, it is dangerous, but not as much as it was. American Don Kellner, for example, has performed 36 000 jumps and he's still with us. US National Safety Council statistics show that in 2001 bee-stings killed 46 Americans, 11 more than sky diving. That being said, sky diving still killed 35 more Americans than table tennis.

THE RUNDOWN

Da Vinci first drew one in the 1480s, Faust Vrančić first flew one in 1783. Jump number one from a moving aeroplane was made in 1913 but the parachute was still thought of primarily (as it had been in the heyday of ballooning) as a rescue device.

By the 1930s it was widely realised that the 'chute might be useful in a war, and not just to save pilots. A new branch of the military was born and during World War Two paratroopers were dropped behind enemy lines—and into trees, onto roads and against the sides of buildings. The problem was that the round parachutes afforded so little control that in some theatres of war military planners calculated on 25 per cent of the dropped troops being injured on landing and therefore unable to participate in the all-important killing others part of the operation.

Jumping out of aeroplanes as a sport didn't gather pace until after World War Two. In 1948 Leo Valentin developed a position—the belly down, spread-eagled arch position then known imaginatively as The Valentin—that enabled divers to maintain stability while freefalling. He also developed techniques for twisting, turning, barrel rolling and for recovering when it all went wrong. Suddenly, freefall became an enjoyable part of the jump rather than a turbulent and risky period merely to be endured before popping the 'chute.

The first Parachuting World Championships were held in 1951 in Yugoslavia, but the contestants were still using round 'chutes. As veteran American jumper Bill Ottley once said, it required black magic to hit a target:

It was Mary Poppins floating through the air. The jumper had to calculate the position of the airplane, wind speed, and other elements. Then he took a deep breath and jumped.

Since the late 1960s parachutes have become more like wings. These square, so-called ram-air 'chutes provide a rigid curved surface thanks to the air pressure inflating a series of chambers. They are highly manoeuvrable, meaning modern parachutists are engaging in something close to controlled flight, not just falling with style.

Parachuting suddenly became safer (for a start, more lift meant softer landings) and more involving. Add the modern Automatic Activation Device (AAD) to ensure the 'chute opened even if the jumper didn't pull the ripcord, and suddenly there was the real risk that sky diving would no longer be classified as dangerous. Fortunately, however, sky divers realised there was a huge variety of new ways in which to ensure their favourite pastime retained its position on the extremity of extreme sport.

One effective way of combating the falling injury rate has been to introduce lighter, smaller parachutes. In the hands of experienced sky divers, these 'high-performance' variants make it possible to swoop near the ground at speeds of 130 kilometres per hour and more. They are spectacular to watch, enormous fun to use and add a whole new level of peril to modern parachuting. (In *Jump! Make your First Skydive Fun and Easy*, author Tom Buchanan cites a wide variety of statistics and concludes the vast majority of accidents during the 1990s involved not novices but 'very experienced skydivers exceeding their own limits'.)

It was a wickedly fast deceleration. I didn't know where I was, which country I was in, it took me a whole minute to collect my thoughts about what was happening.

Then there are the other modern variations on standard sky diving: accuracy contests (rather like using your body as a dart and the world as your dartboard), formation work, speed freefalling, freestyle and sky surfing, to name but a few.

Stacked canopy formation is also known as CRW (pronounced crew, it stands for Canopy Relative Work). Each jumper hooks his legs into the lines of the jumper below, making a stack of sky divers sometimes numbering as many as 80. It looks very pretty as long as they don't get their legs and lines tangled up, or their canopies collide and collapse and they end up flat-packed.

Freestyle involves performing a series of gymnastic manoeuvres before opening the 'chute. Freestylers usually wear baggy jumpsuits to increase wind resistance, and therefore control. Because freestyle has a strong aesthetic

People always distort the risk because it is an unnatural concept to jump out of a plane. But if you understand the risks and do everything to mitigate them, it is what I'd describe as very safe.

element, they often forgo helmets and even shoes. Pointing head-down can increase the falling speed to 260 kilometres per hour, 'sitting' can slow it by 40 kilometres per hour, and a belly-to-ground position pulls it back below 200 kilometres per hour. Varying their speed enables freestylers to move over and under each other. Collisions are a risk; even though the parachutists are moving in clear air, a collision involving a 50 kilometres per hour difference in speed is still a 50 kilometres per hour collision and enough to knock someone out cold—or worse.

In the late 1980s, Frenchman Joel Cruciani modified a small surfboard, mounted snowboard-style bindings on it and invented the sport of sky surfing. The 'surfboards' soon became smaller—somewhere in between a skateboard or snowboard—which made them more controllable. Surfers could achieve speeds of nearly 200 kilometres per hour, in a variety of directions, though sky surfing's particular challenge is that the board catches so much wind it can spin its rider out of control, or tangle with the 'chute.

Sky surfing became competitive by the 1990s, as a team sport. One team member surfs, the other films. The team is marked for degree of difficulty of the moves (such as the 'Helicopter Spin', which involves spinning the board rotor-like while upside down) and the quality of the filming.

For some sky divers it is all about speed, which usually involves wearing special slippery suits and going for the ground head-first, with arms and legs tucked in tightly. Australian Ashley Crick didn't start sky diving until 1996, but was world freestyle champion in 1999 and 2000. He also won the World Cup of Speed Skydiving in Lapalisse, France, with a speed of 491 kilometres per hour measured over a kilometre. During his fall the peak speed exceeded 500 kilometres per hour, faster than any other non-motorised sport (and the vast majority of motorised sports, too).

'There is a massive amount of pressure and extreme noise,' Crick says of travelling through air at such a speed. In a normal sky dive the air feels more like a liquid than a gas, he says, but 'when you are hitting 500 kilometres per hour it is feeling like a solid, like you are pressing against a wooden bench.'

The speed sky diving position, presenting just your head and shoulders to the wind, is very unstable and even moving a few fingers into the airstream will slow the sky diver down 50 kilometres per hour. He or she can be badly bruised by the air pressure, and divers have suffered dislocated shoulders as a result of the deceleration caused by changing their position at the end of the speed run. To achieve maximum velocity you can't even look at the ground—you need to peer across at the horizon. Crick points out that most speed sky divers have two different altimeters that beep in their ear, and a light that flashes at a predetermined height:

> *The main risk is that you are not height aware. If you realise too late and try to open the parachute at speed it will probably disintegrate. The second greatest risk is that your parachute comes out of its container because of the forces prior to slowing down.*

This happened once to Crick at 412 kilometres per hour. He was shaken, but managed to escape injury:

> *It was a wickedly fast deceleration. I didn't know where I was, which country I was in, it took me a whole minute to collect my thoughts about what was happening. It was like something massive grabbing you, but surprisingly the parachute held together.*

On the subject of sky diving safety, Crick says:

People always distort the risk because it is an unnatural concept to jump out of a plane. But if you understand what the risks are in sky diving and do everything you can to mitigate them, it is what I'd describe as very safe.

In 3000 jumps, Crick has had one serious injury: he broke his back and split his foot 'in two' in an accident in Spain, having failed to stay mainly on the plain (crosswinds blew him too close to a house which cut the airflow to his small ram 'chute). He dropped the last ten metres like a stone. Crick said there was an upside—the two months he spent in hospital was the only time he has ever slowed down.

Now, perhaps the most exciting new variation of sky diving is wingsuits. These were used for the world's highest BASE jump in 2006 and for the world sky diving distance record (over 20 kilometres), blurring the line between BASE jumping, sky diving and hang gliding.

A wingsuit has spans of double-layered material with air pockets that inflate to create wings between the wearer's limbs. These wings enable the sky diver to slow their vertical descent to about 60 kilometres per hour but increase the horizontal velocity to 180 kilometres per hour. By moving their arms and legs, wingsuit wearers can bank like an aeroplane.

POSSIBLE INJURIES

Broken fingers, toes and limbs. Broken everything else.

Joe Kittinger was a young daredevil who almost killed himself on several occasions racing his hydroplane speedboat. In 1949 he joined the US Air Force, which generously took over the job of trying to kill him at the tax-payer's expense. In 1957 it sent Kittinger up in a balloon 29 500 metres above the Earth. This was touted as the first time a man had been in space. Two years later Kittinger was up again, at a slightly more modest 23 287 metres, but this time he was slated to jump out. Wearing a pressurised suit, he leapt out of the open gondola and headed for Earth, but started rotating at 120 revolutions per minute, almost spin-drying his organs. Although he was soon unconscious, Kittinger's prototype 'chute deployed automatically, and three weeks later he was back at it again. In 1960 he sky dived from a record 31 300 metres—31.3 kilometres—above the Earth. 'It was a helluva long way down, but the quickest way to get there,' he said laconically. Kittinger was in freefall for just over four-and-a-half minutes. There is some conjecture about the maximum speed he reached before being slowed by the denser air closer to Earth. Contemporary reports said he hit 614 miles per hour or 988 kilometres per hour, but Kittinger and the National Museum of the United States Air Force later claimed his maximum speed was 714 miles per hour (1149 kilometres per hour) and that he broke the speed of sound.

* **André-Jacques Garnerin.** *In 1797 this Frenchman jumped from a hot air balloon that was floating about 1000 metres above Parc Monceau in Paris. The secret of his survival was a foldable silk parachute. Up until then, parachutes had been made of cloth or canvas stretched across large wooden frames. Garnerin soon improved his compact parachute by adding slots for better stability. In 1798 his wife Jeanne-Genevieve became the world's first female parachutist.*

* **Rod Pack.** *This stuntman jumped out of a plane in 1965 without a parachute and was handed one in freefall by another sky diver, who had jumped out of a different plane. Pack exited at 4500 metres, received the chute at 3000 metres, spent 1200 metres fitting it and was finally in a position to rip the chute at just over 1000 metres. It was all done in front of the cameras of the magazine* **Life**—*a title which, for Pack, could have so easily been a misnomer.*

* **Jay Stokes.** *In 2006 this 50-year-old American broke his own eccentric world record by making 640 parachute jumps in one 24-hour period. To do this, Stokes had to land as closely as possible to the taxiing aircraft, shed his 'chute pretty well at the moment he touched down and run to the already moving plane, while assistants helped strap on a new 'chute en route. Stokes had three planes on the go and 20 assistants. He spent just eight seconds on the ground each time. 'When you are doing this,' he said, 'you question yourself "Why am I even here?".' He probably wasn't the only one asking.*

* **Rob Harris.** *A Californian credited with being the first to truly master sky surfing. He became a double world champion but, in late 1995, was killed while filming a James Bond-type television commercial for Mountain Dew soft drink. Harris's 'chute became tangled and the reserve didn't open in time. The ad is still shown in the United States, though the footage used is from earlier jumps.*

The big drop: 500 kilometres per hour is possible thanks to slippery suits, plenty of height and great bravery. The two most notable sensations at that speed, says Ashley Crick, are massive pressure and extreme noise.

Photo: Alamy stock photography

ACKNOWLEDGEMENTS

Thanks to the many people who kindly spoke to me about their sport, offered background information or advice, helped with photos, or merely pointed me in the right direction: Tanya Streeter, Greg Mortimer, Frank Evans, Espen Bredesen, Wayne Gardner, Dr Glenn Singleman, Herbert Nitsch, Joe Bugner, Tracie Max Sachs, Ashley Crick, Bill Moyes, Rosco McGlashan, Patrick Musimu, Glynne Bowsher, Tony Armstrong, Sue Werner, Ross Clarke-Jones, Maseeh Nasheet, Richard Noble, Lisa Evans, Bill Fryer, Jon Leven, Annemarie Friedrich, Tim Cayer, Tim Hardman, Lawrence Legend, Margaux Nissen-Gray, Joey Zuber, Dave Auld, Michael Milton, David Kirke, Michael Carroll, Laura McLachlan, Dr Whitney Azoy, Nikki Vasiliadis, Tim Elliot, Mai-Lis Degerstrom, Glenn Morrison, Peter McKay, Damian Davis, Penni Lewer, Wing Commander Andy Green and Miran Tepeš. If wrong turns were taken, the fault is entirely mine. Thanks also to the crew at Allen & Unwin and its shiny new Arena imprint: Jude McGee, Louise Thurtell, Catherine Taylor, Jane Alexander, Justine O'Donnell, Andrew Hawkins and all the others who contributed to producing this book.

Tony Davis
June 2007

The wonder of
unpowered flight.
Wings over Aspen,
Colorado.

Photo: Christian Pondella/
Red Bull Photofiles

238

Greg Mortimer on K2, perhaps the toughest mountain on Earth. 'There is something in man,' said Everest pioneer George Mallory, 'that responds to the challenge of the mountain.'

Photo Greg Mortimer/Aurora Expeditions

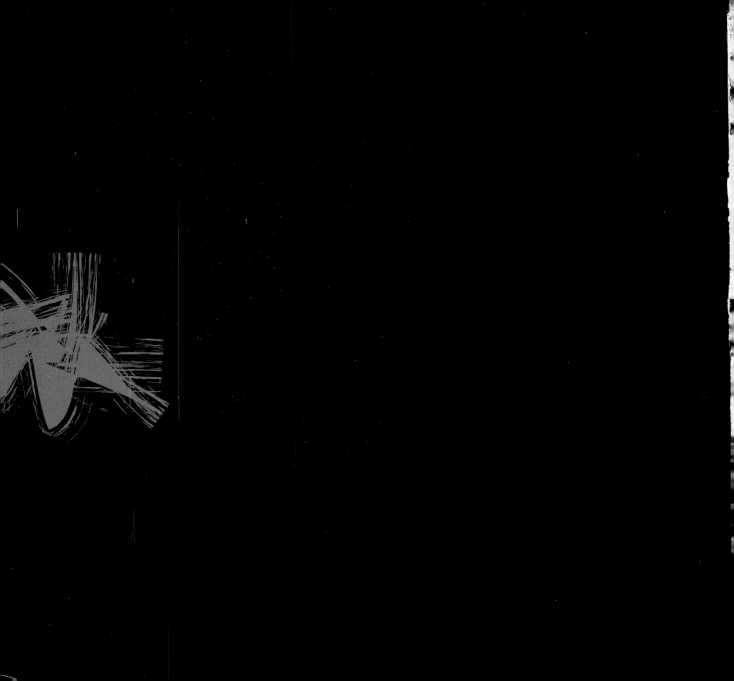